WHAT COPS TALK ABOUT OVER COFFEE

Volume I

Compiled by
ROBERT ROGALSKI
Regimental #24556 - Retired Sergeant - Royal Canadian Mounted Police

What Cops Talk About Over Coffee
Copyright © 2020 by Robert Rogalski

All rights reserved. No part of this publication may be reproduced, distributed, or transmitted in any form or by any means, including photocopying, recording, or other electronic or mechanical methods, without the prior written permission of the author, except in the case of brief quotations embodied in critical reviews and certain other non-commercial uses permitted by copyright law.

Submission of material for consideration in this book, whether in writing, print or by any other means, constitutes the waiving of all rights to said material. All submissions past, present, and future become the property of Bob Rogalski.

Tellwell Talent
www.tellwell.ca

ISBN
978-0-2288-2576-0 (Paperback)
978-0-2288-2577-7 (eBook)

*A Collection of memories
from the 1950's to 2012.*

Table of Contents

Dedication & Acknowledgements vii
Preface ix
My Story - Introduction xiii

Chapter 1 Depot Training Flashbacks 1
Chapter 2 First Posting 13
Chapter 3 Memorable Drunks 25
Chapter 4 Driving Incidents 33
Chapter 5 That close call 37
Chapter 6 Partners I Remember 49
Chapter 7 Courtroom Memories 61
Chapter 8 Staffing Interviews 69
Chapter 9 Keeping Sane On Midnight Shift 75
Chapter 10 Practical Jokes Played 83
Chapter 11 Applicants - Interviews 97
Chapter 12 Gone Are The Days When 101
Chapter 13 Extra Ordinary Duty 111
Chapter 14 Quotes On Assessments 121
Chapter 15 On Patrol 123
Chapter 16 Embarrassing Moments 189
Chapter 17 You Had To Be There 205

DEFINITIONS OF ABBREVIATED TERMS USED IN THIS BOOK

Force.........	Referred to as the RCMP
Cst..........	Constable
S/Cst.........	Special Constable
Cpl..........	Corporal
Sgt..........	Sergeant
CPIC.........	Canadian Police Information Centre
NCIC.........	National Crime Index Centre
PC..........	Police Cruiser
OCC.........	Operational Communications Centre
Depot.........	Royal Canadian Mounted Police Training Academy –Regina Saskatchewan
NCO.........	Non-Commissioned Officer
CABS.........	Computer Aided Booking System
J-3..........	Prisoner In Custody
MDT.........	Mobile Data Terminal
CPU..........	Crime Prevention Unit
GIS..........	General Investigation Section

Dedication & Acknowledgements

To my wife Shirley & two sons, Ian & Jason: Thank you for your support and love as you accompanied me through my adventures in my career.

My hobby of collecting stories and anecdotes from peace officers throughout my career include my own experiences. Most of the sources from RCMP, City Police, Federal & Provincial agencies remain anonymous however a few have requested their names stand as contributors. Individuals in some stories have some of their names changed to protect the identity of those involved. It became obvious to me these stories have probably been repeated to peers or others over coffee or during social conversation. Some contributors have long since passed away knowing full well that I promised them I would document their memories in a collection for the general public to read.

This collection is dedicated to the many Peace Officers who have served their departments well and who have in some cases never been given appropriate recognition for a job well done in their careers. It was interesting to see how quickly members would reflect on the first memory of an event as they looked at the many chapter headings I laid out before them.

The first person who inspired me to take on this venture was Corporal Bob Teather, a colleague of mine, who had written a number of books about police culture in the past. I want to thank my youngest son, Jason, as well as Gertie Attfield and Olive (Ollie) Hunter who are close friends who did some editing and gave me good feedback on how the general public might view the content of this book. Many thanks to those who provided encouragement and ideas for me to continue my quest. In order to keep the contributing participants anonymous, I used the personal pronoun "I" or "We" in all the stories. Some contributors wished to have their names stand as contributors. To further clarify, I wasn't the officer in all the stories.

Special acknowledgement to those contributors of sketches and cartoons with their own version of policing. They include, Graham Muir, Murray Macaulay, Don Ormiston. I want to thank Adrian's at the Airport restaurant in Langley, B.C. for providing the table setting for the book cover. Photo by Tim Linsdell.

ENJOY

R.J. (Bob) Rogalski – Retired Sgt. Regimental #24556

(Known amongst many of his friends and colleagues as "Rogy").

Preface

Every police officer has stories for a book in him or her, or at least a chapter. One of the interesting things about police work is the high level of privacy with which most members treat the work they do and the individuals they deal with.. that is unless they are having coffee, or lunch with their counterparts on the job. If the walls could talk at Tim Horton's, or Boston Pizza, there would be a never- ending source of material for 'CSI Wherever' or 'The Rookie'.. Stories are shared about the last call, told in the moments stolen to gag down a few calories before heading off to answer the next one, or over a "beverage" at the end of shift.

This book is an outstanding collection that sheds light on what most of us call shop talk; first hand accounts of the everyday drama that is part of the amazing work done every day by the men and women whose responsibility it is to stand between the citizens of Canada and the violence that is, unfortunately, a part of today's landscape.

In small towns and large cities across Canada, both real drama and comedy occur on a daily basis, witnessed by members of the police community, who, by their choice of professions, become part of the plot that unfolds. Most stories go untold. Many others are reproduced in reports and court documents, but seldom with the perspective, context and reality of the moment lived and recalled amongst friends.

This book will shine that light and allow you a seldom seen peek at how it really went down and how it really felt…. I have enjoyed this glimpse into the memoirs of those who contributed and I know that you will also find it an interesting view, whether or not you have had first-hand experience in police work. These accounts are both heart warming and humorous, some are frightening; others offer some insight into the human spirit…. They are real stories told by real heroes…. I hope you enjoy the collection as much as I have.

Bev Busson, RCMP Commissioner – retired,
C.O.M., O.B.C., LL.B, LL.D(Hon)UCFV, LL.D(Hon)SFU.

PREFACE

The stories and memories compiled herein will resonate with all former and serving police officers. They serve as glimpses and snapshots in time and capture the broad range of a police officer's experience. While reading these vignettes, I was struck by how much things have changed and also by how much some things never change.

Police officers, I think, are a unique breed. We are exposed to the entire spectrum of the human condition - the good, the bad and the ugly. Through that exposure a bond is created between police officers that can only truly be understood by those in the profession.

Reading these stories will certainly trigger memories of your own experiences, perhaps memories you haven't thought of for many years. Enjoy!

W. Fraser MacRae, Assistant Commissioner,
Officer in Charge RCMP - Surrey Detachment

PREFACE

Bob Rogalski has done a great service with his book of anecdotes and memorial tidbits.

I practiced law in Kamloops from mid 1969 until the end of 1975 with a fair amount of my practice being in the Provincial Court, Criminal Division. I remember Bob as I remember several other RCMP members of that time and they were all well liked and respected by Bench and

Bar alike. Practicing criminal law in a small centre breeds a good deal of bonhomie amongst Bench, Bar and Police and it wasn't a rare sight to see all three having a brew in the Canadian Inn Beer Parlour; in off duty moments, of course.

The Courtroom, indeed the entire criminal process being such a serious matter breeds its own kind of humour, not quite a "gallows humour", but close. It often comes about as a release from some of the very bad parts, such as dealing with grisly murders, molestation of children, hit and run cases and other unsavory matters which make it difficult to keep one's perspective.

The Bench, Bar and Police have this in common: outsiders wonder just what sort of people they are in real life. Are they always as serious as when we see them? They must let their hair down sometimes, what do they talk about?

Bob skillfully lets all peep, invisibly, inside the coffee shop and other gathering places to learn how very human cops really are.

Bob's many delightful vignettes will much amuse the reader and for those involved in these matters, provide very special reminiscences they can all relate to, even though they might not have actually been there themselves.

Rafe Mair

The late Rafe Mair was a lawyer, former cabinet minister in the BC government, writer and Hall of Fame broadcaster who lived in Lions Bay B.C.

* * * *

My Story - Introduction

Follow the career and journey of regimental # 24556, retired Sergeant Robert Rogalski, more commonly known by his peers and colleagues as "Rogy". My journey covers almost 50 years of involvement with the policing establishment and includes 28 years as a regular member of the Royal Canadian Mounted Police. After retiring from the RCMP in 1995, I established myself as a training consultant and for over 20 years facilitated in the delivery of field training officer courses for the RCMP and other Federal and Provincial policing agencies across Canada.

I grew up in rural Killaly, Saskatchewan and was the youngest of five children in our farming family. My early years of growing up involved a lot of imagination. I remember my father and brothers listening to the radio programs in the evenings which included the favorite western themes of 'The lone Ranger; Hop Along Cassidy and Cops and Robbers type programs like 'Boston Blacky'. All these programs had me putting my imagination to work and pretending I was one of the characters.

After graduating from high school in 1965, I joined the RCMP on February 06, 1966. I had broken service with The RCMP as my first 3.5 years were periods of service doing general duty police work in Edmonton, Viking, Fort McMurray and Fort Chipewyan Detachments in Alberta.

During the latter part of 1969 and into 1970 I stayed active working on the family farm assisting my two other brothers in clearing land they had purchased to expand their grain farming operations. It was in the Fall of 1970 that I met my wife whom I had known since high school. At that time I was in the middle of my application to get back into the RCMP and was successful to once again rejoin the RCMP in March of 1971. I was transferred to Kamloops, B.C. and spent 9 years working general duty along with some plain clothes experience. I was referred to as a "Retread" because of my previous service. We got married in August of 1972 and were later blessed with two sons.

In 1979 I was transferred to Prince Rupert Detachment where housing was at a premium and the interest rates for mortgages were at 16% putting a lot of strain on anyone putting money into a primary residence. I recall stopping in Williams Lake, B.C. on my house-hunting trip and saw a small poem on the bathroom wall. It was a fitting statement to my situation. It read "Life is like a shit sandwich – the more bread you got the less shit you eat". We settled into Prince Rupert without difficulty as our two sons were very young. We worked hard and played hard as detachment members were a close knit group. There were lots of opportunities for social activities amongst the various professional people who worked in the community.

Between 1981 and 1985 I was posted to Depot Division, Regina, Saskatchewan where I enjoyed four years as an academic instructor teaching law and operational applications to groom new recruits for the field. This period of time was very rewarding as I witnessed many recruits pass through their training with a strong career ahead of them.

In 1985 I was transferred to Surrey Detachment where the next few years provided me experience working in community policing and as a Training N.C.O. I eventually was promoted to Sergeant working out of "E" Division Head Quarters, Vancouver and was responsible for the delivery of the Recruit Field Training Program. I retired from the RCMP on 1995 August 2nd and set myself up as a training consultant, teaching Field Training Officer courses for the RCMP and other policing agencies in Canada.

My career allowed me to gather a collection of memories from police officers across Canada and outside jurisdictions which included firsthand accounts of situations they have encountered in their careers from the 1950's to 2012. Contributions from RCMP, city police, Federal and Provincial law enforcement agencies were collected over a 30 year period and pose as a snapshot of the type of conversations or "shop talk" two police officers might have during their coffee break. These accounts are both heartwarming and humorous, some are frightening while others offer some insight into the human spirit. They are real stories told by real heroes.

R.J. Rogalski

CHAPTER #1

Depot Training Flashbacks

Every police officer who reflects on their initial training period has fond memories of specific incidents or experiences that stand out.

» » Surviving in the Swimming Pool » »

My first recollection of training at the RCMP Depot Division, Regina, was in the swimming pool in 1966. Some swimming instructor, a Sgt. yelling at me that if I stick my head under the water and wiggle my ears, I would probably get further. The tourist gallery burst into laughter as they could see I had very large protruding ears.

» » Stable Duties » »

During equitation training on Saturday afternoon our troop marches in to feed the horses. One of my troop mates clears his throat and spits on the concrete floor depositing what appeared to look like an oyster on the floor. "HALT" was the scream of the stable master. "Who was responsible for that?" The troop mate answered and waited for sentencing. "CST., get down on the floor, sit in it and make like the WATUSI..... needless to say the floor was clean, my troop mate wore the evidence on his breaches and the horses were fed.

» »   Horse Barns - First Inspection   » »

After cleaning the stables I had to stand directly behind the horse I had just groomed. Being a seasoned farm boy didn't have me too uptight until a senior troop member next to me whispered out of the side of his mouth "Whatever you do, don't move - a gun is going off". Sure enough, seconds later a British Lee-Enfield .303 caliber rifle shot off a blank round. The sound echoed throughout the barn and it felt like it shook the building. The horses responded with a jump and seemed agitated. A few members stepped back from their attention positions. The stable master focused on one of the recruits just steps from where I was and yelled out "What the %$&# are you moving for? - do you want me to phone your mother - get down and do 25." I was lucky. I guess this was all supposed to build character, and who knows, maybe it did.

» »   The Parade Square   » »

While on the parade square the Sgt. Major blurts out "You - with the big ears - tuck your hands in for God's sake." I couldn't figure out how he could pick me out of 400 guys on the Parade Square. 15 years later I shared my flashback with that same Sgt. Major, now a retired Inspector. He smiled and said "What you didn't know is that 400 other constables on the square thought the same thing and corrected themselves as well.

» »   The Drill Hall   » »

The Drill Cpl points his pacer wand into the chest of a young constable and states "Cst., there is a piece of shit on the end of my stick." The young recruit quickly replies "Not on my end Corporal."

» »   Something is Not Catholic Here!   » »

I was supervising an operational training exercise where a suspect's vehicle was placed just outside a building with a girl behind the driver's seat. The door to the drill hall was ajar and in the back of the vehicle were two jackets etc, left by culprits who were placed within the building pretending to be break & enter artists. As the recruits approached this complaint related to a suspicious vehicle, they followed all procedures taught but couldn't get the big picture. While they were trying to grasp what might be happening with this scenario, I can recall asking one of the young French speaking recruits if he was able to get a good picture of what was going on. He remarked "I don't know Cpl, but something's not Catholic here!".

At this time the two suspects fled from the drill hall just in front of the suspect's vehicle and the chase was on. One suspect was caught by one of the members while the other controlled the girl and the suspect's vehicle.

This scenario was one of my favourite because it created a wide variety of reactions from members who were investigating this complaint. On a number of occasions the Police transport was taken by the suspects who circled back after leading the members away from the scene. Rest assured these young officers would have taken their experiences with them into the field, and react more cautiously next time.

» »   **Getting his point across**   » »

While observing a young French recruit struggle through his first investigation I tried to encourage him to make sure that his suspect knew exactly what he was doing as an investigator. I watched him read the police warning from the card provided in his notebook. His French accent seemed to take over when the suspect interrupted and asked "What the hell does that all mean?" The recruit replied as best he could "Dat means, If you want, you can shut up!!!"

» »   **Call it the way you see it**   » »

A young French-speaking recruit was giving it his best shot in report writing. He was the main investigator of a break and enter complaint of a grocery store. His criminal report started with confidence until he came to describe the scene. "I went on patrol of a report of break and enter and I came to Queen Street to look at the grocery store. It was obvious that her rear had been entered so I continued my investigation."

»» I know what you mean »»

During a C.P.R. First Aid training class - a Fisheries member from Newfoundland was being tested for his C.P.R. skills. This was in response to finding an unconscious lady on the floor. "Hay lady, lady, you O.K? Then he points to me and says "You, you know where you're to, go get an ambulance and come where we're at." I had been given my first lesson in how a Newfoundlander might express himself under stress.

»» The Dreaded Law Exams »»

While teaching Law and administering Law Exams I would correct their papers and made a note of some of the answers recruits would provide. Recruits were very focussed on their new environment and subsequently gave some unique answers. A few choice answers collected include:

Q: What is LIMITATION OF ACTION?

A: The time it takes to lay an informant.

The answer I was looking for was: the time limit scheduled in law to lay a charge against someone.

Q: How do you open court?

A: Turn the knob and open the door., or With a key.

The answer I was looking for was: "Order in the Court, please rise – Justice Brown presiding".

Q: Where is H.Q. for Depot Division?

A: The Guardroom.

The answer I was looking for was in fact the Training Academy at Regina, Saskatchewan. Most recruits only could think of the "Guardroom", which was the central reporting station for all recruits.

Q: Quote in the Administration Manual where it states "Members are not allowed to smoke in uniform?"

A: Don't worry Cpl., I don't smoke.

Q: What is ARRAIGNMENT?

A: Rain with mint in it.

The answer I was looking was: Bringing a suspect before the Court to answer to a charge.

Q: In using force to affect a lawful arrest what necessary steps should you take in your technique to avoid allegations of excessive force?

A: (1) Have witnesses.
    (2) Take or offer to transport to a doctor.
    (3) Be sure to give him an option.
    (4) Gently
    (5) Get rough
    (6) As much as is necessary to get the job done.

The answer I was looking for was to use as much force as necessary.

» » My blanket caught on fire » »

While in Regina in the Spring of 1983 and training with (F-troop) S/Cst. I had the fortune of being in the same block as an Indigenous troop who were good sports. One of our instructors who was known for his sense of humour and a member serving at Regina Air Section thought it would be a good idea to set off the fire alarm at 2:00 AM. We were aroused from our beds by the Duty NCO indicating there was a bomb threat and everyone had to be accounted for in front of "C" block. We were tired because we had just finished our going away party from Depot and were not particularly fussy about getting up. Some of us just jumped into a pair of P.J's. while others just put on a pair of long blues (uniform pants). After collecting in front of C block the duty NCO appeared to be taking a head count when our Regina Air Section troop mate drove up and took a picture of us standing around on the windy and cold, snowy sidewalk. We knew we were taken advantage of at this point. Later I spoke to one of the guys in the Indigenous troop who demonstrated the mood of being a bit ticked off and upset over being awakened from a sound sleep by a false alarm. He said "Sorry guys, I was sending a message home to my family and the blanket I was using caught on fire".

» »   Putting your foot in your mouth   » »

I was the troop counsellor for a group of young men who represented a wide variety of characters. The troop had 24 bilingual members and only 8 unilingual members. The first day in the dorm I was looked upon as the counsellor to assist in the troops' early stages of development. My opening remarks actually created more feedback to me regarding my attitude towards certain people, and to date some still recall the remarks. I recall making statements to the effect that those speaking French as a first language will probably find it hard to digest the atmosphere around training because everything will be done in English. Then I went on to say, "For the rest of you white guys" and said what I had to. This one statement came back to haunt me as the months progressed as some took offence to same. I kept reminding those who jokingly brought it to my attention that what they were about to face after leaving Depot would be far more severe than what I was dishing out.

» » Arousing a suspect » »

In the mid 1980's a female member is giving evidence in a mock court case dealing with a care and control impaired driving suspect. I was acting as the defence lawyer and heard her evidence as follows. "I arrived at the scene and found a male asleep behind the wheel of this car. The keys were still in the ignition". The prosecutor asked "What did you do then, Constable?"

Her reply: "I attempted to arouse this man".

My first question to the constable as a defence lawyer was "You say that you attempted to arouse this man - Did you enjoy that, Constable?"

The teaching point here was watch out how you articulate giving your evidence so that what is said is not construed to mean something else.

» » Oops – Forgot something » »

While in training at Depot in the spring of 1969 I recall having a leisurely swim on a Sunday evening when we didn't have Sgt. Canning on our backs and telling us there were three types of swimming stokes; the right one, the wrong one and the RCMP one. I was at the pool with some of my troop mates one Sunday evening and it was normal to see a lot of other outside staff members and families in the pool during this same time. This was a free time for swimming but also a time when recruits were expected to attend for extra swimming to improve their skills.

The swimming instructors had a hard and fast rule during training that if any recruit came into the pool area, they were to ensure they showered before they entered the pool area If they attended after training hours they were to announce their arrival at the duty desk when they entered the main pool area. On this evening the pool was busy with families laughing and enjoying the water and their activities.

I was standing on the low diving board and could not believe my eyes when I observed a fellow recruit from another troop enter the pool area. His drill instructor would have been proud; he was walking erect with his shoulders back but he forgot one thing - his bathing suit. He was stark naked and from his strut, proud of it.

He marched to the duty desk and promptly came to attention announcing his name and troop number. The pool became hushed as the pool attendant glanced up to notice the shortcomings of the recruit. He could hardly believe his eyes. He simply pointed and with that our prominent member of Troop 7 quickly 'exited stage left'. I guess he was in such a rush to show up for extra swimming that he had completely forgotten to put on his bathing suit after showering. We all had a good laugh after he quickly departed for the dressing room. For quite some time after this, I recall this member being teased with the nick-name "stubby". Years later I met and worked for this member's father and enjoyed telling him the story at the expense of his son's embarrassment.

» »   Noon Day Parade Roll Call   » »

The noonday parade at Depot Division in Regina is enjoyed by many tourists and public who attend to watch the activities on Base. It is February in mid-Winter. The temperature seemed like 40 below zero and the wind was howling at about 40 kph. Snowflakes were flying through the crisp frigid air. The spectator stands are empty and there are two troops on parade. Our band consists of one member and a snare drum. Each troop on parade has one Corporal who conducts a quick inspection and role call before the parade protocol is complete.

The normal parade formalities are done and now it is time for the Sergeant Major to check to see if all recruits on parade are accounted for. This is what I heard.

Sergeant Major: "#1 Troop – report".

Cpl standing in front of #1 Troop: "All accounted for –Sir!"

Sergeant Major: "#2 Troop"

Cpl standing in front of #2 Troop: "One not accounted for – Sir!" and continues to say "I called the name Arnold ZIFFLE and no one answered!"

Sergeant Major: "Have that person report to me at 4:30 today" "Parade will advance in troop column, etc."

Note: A popular T.V. Series at that time called "Green Acres" had a pet pig named "Arnold Ziffle", which made this all the more hilarious.

I saw the Corporal leading the first troop laughing so hard as the parade got underway that he could hardly control himself. The more he laughed, the more the remainder of the rest of the troops joined in trying to still look professional as they marched off the parade square.

CHAPTER #2

First Posting

» »   Reaction to Train Whistle?   » »

In rural Alberta, near the farming community of Viking, I recall driving down a rural back road and approaching a C.N. railroad crossing. It's about 3:30 a.m. and subconsciously I'm thinking – What if the C.N. Mainliner comes through here like it usually does at about 80 mph without me seeing it?" I'm doing about 45-50 mph. Suddenly the tone alert comes on over the police radio – "KSH.@X KSH "@ ...XJK 88" from Edmonton sub-division etc.etc. this is a stolen car bulletin". The tone alert was loud enough and to a degree similar to an air horn. This triggered my reactions to thinking it was the horn from the C.N. Mainliner coming through as I was just about to cross the tracks. I recall hitting the brakes so hard just before that crossing that the police car wound up stopping sideways on the road in front of the tracks. I called it a night after that and packed in the shift.

» »   Learning about patience   » »

I'm stationed at Viking, Alberta, a small two man rural posting in the late 1960's. A man phones in that his car was stolen from downtown. It's about 4 p.m. and I've got my hat on to go. On this call. The Cpl. in charge is sitting and typing a report yet doesn't seem too concerned and I'm having an ulcer about getting into the P.C. (Police Cruiser) and heading out to investigate. My Cpl. suggests we should sit put for a few minutes.

Sure enough, not five minutes later the same man phones back advising that he had just misplaced his car across the street. No further action taken. This was my first lesson in not getting too carried away with my career.

» »   **Pull over**   » »

My first posting gave me the opportunity to apply what I had learned in training. I was anxious to try out the various tools and equipment installed in the police cruiser, including use of the communication system. I head out onto Highway 14 and start checking any vehicle that comes within my location. It is mid-afternoon and traffic was light. The locals I check are either farmers or business people on their way to the city. They all seem respectful and produce the necessary documents. This gives me a chance to introduce myself as the new cop in town. All goes well for a few checks as my confidence level improves. I am 15 miles out of town and begin to notice vehicles way ahead of me quickly pull over to the side of the road as I casually cruise down the highway. I do a few road side checks and head back to the office. As I pull up in front of the Detachment the reflection of the flashing red stop lights could be seen in the large picture window of the Detachment office. I realized I had not switched off the emergency lights after my last couple of stops. No wonder everyone had pulled over giving me the room to pass.

» »   **I'll look into that**   » »

From time to time I had the opportunity to take a person from our community on a 'ride along' experience. I had met a fellow who was my age and who expressed an interest in coming out one evening to see what kind of patrols we might conduct. It was Friday evening and not much was happening. I was on patrol on a rural back road and spotted an empty case of beer in the middle of the road. It was an overcast night so I pulled the police cruiser close enough to shine the spotlight on the case of beer and commenced to show my friend how my .38 calibre revolver functioned. I emptied the weapon out and reloaded to allow my friend to try and hit the target. There was a farm yard about 3/4 mile away. I heard horses running in a nearby pasture as we were shooting.

Two days later as I am going to get the mail at the local post office, I meet this irate farmer who tells me that some idiot was out his way a few nights ago with a spot light shooting at something on the road. He told me his horses ran home, tore his fence down and his own kids, who were sleeping in a tent, got scared and came running into the house. I reassured this poor man that I would make some enquiries and see if I could determine who was in the area that night. I did not have the guts to tell this man I was the culprit. Luckily, my Cpl was away on leave and I made sure I was unsuccessful in determining who might have been the suspects. Case concluded.

» » Marijuana Lesson » »

In the mid-1960s only the very basic information on illegal drugs was taught to recruits going through training. Things like *flower children* and *Hippie* stood out for those of us who were far too naive to even capture a hope of getting a good understanding of what was happening on the streets. We had a glimpse of what drug addicts would use and only saw marijuana in picture format. While stationed at Fort McMurray in the fall of 1968 one of the boys on shift came walking into the office at about 11:30 p.m. indicating that if we wanted to know what marijuana smelled like after it was smoked, we should hustle down to the local pizza joint and take a walk through. The whole shift took intermittent turns to stroll through and get a whiff of this new substance hitting town. It scared the hell out of me because when I joined the force nobody sat me down and pointed out what possible ramifications such a drug would have on policing. How things have changed since then.

» » Becoming a Reserve Constable » »

As a Reserve Constable with the Vancouver Police Department, I was always enthusiastic about my turn at a "Practical", the term used for patrol duties at the Department. The term 'ride-a-long' was set aside for unarmed civilians out to see what was going on. We were trained to be better than that.

During training, it was reinforced many times how important it was to be professional at all times when representing the Force, the City and the Reserve program. This put a good face on the Reserve program and never hurt your own situation when the stuff hit the fan. These are a few of the stories from my six years as a Reserve Constable.

» »   First Patrol Shift   » »

Being part of the Vancouver Police Reserve Force was exciting, but in the beginning a bit nerve wracking too. I had never been part of an organization where you are in uniform in public, unless you count the Boy Scouts!

To ease into it, I felt the best thing to do was pick a potentially slow time, and maybe do the shift with someone I already knew. This would help take the first day jitters away.

During training I had met Brian. He was 6 foot plus, built like a brick you know what. Soon after meeting, I discovered that his wife was a regular member with the VPD. Over the course of our eight month training period, I had occasion to meet her a couple times and thought that if she was willing, I would set up my first official practical shift with her. It would work well as she knew all about the reserve program and our training. No surprises from either side.

It turned out that she worked out of the old Cambie office and through the course of her shift work, did the occasional Sunday early car shift. This was the extra car on the road that covered early morning shift change. It was a 5a.m. start on a Sunday morning. What other time would be so quiet.. perfect for my first time in uniform.

The shift went as well as I had expected with most of our time being the security company alarm response team checking all the homes in the affluent southwest side of the city. Just before the end of the shift we got a call of a possible break & enter in progress. Finally, some action!

We made our way to the back lane of the address provided and got out of the car. Walking up the lane, we spot a fellow on the back porch of a home, completely out of place for the neighbourhood. We approached the individual and asked him what he was doing. His story was not making sense. We asked him to join us so we could figure out what was going on. He came out to the lane and we started the interrogation. His story was all over the place, but he insisted he knew the people that lived in the house.

My partner figured the best thing to do was ask the resident if that was the case, and told me to stay there with the suspect, who was at this point not yet in any type of restraints. She was going to the house to see if there was anybody there who could confirm the suspect's story.

As she walked away, my mind is going a hundred miles an hour. I could feel my heart beating in my chest. I am guarding my first suspect. Should I put cuffs on him? Protocol said he should be in cuffs and searched. Would he let me? Should I do it? What happens if he should decide to leave? These and a hundred other questions are running through my mind at 100 miles per hour.

At that moment, the suspect starts talking. He says he doesn't want to stay. Sure enough, my worst fears are coming to life. I am going to lose my first suspect. I tell him he has to stay. He asks why? I don't have the right to stop him so he should just go he says. I say until we get the story straight, he has to stay put. He again says he doesn't want to.

During training, you are taught to look for signs that your suspect is about to do the unexpected. His body language is yelling at me. My heart is beating faster than ever before and I figure the fight is going to be on at any moment.

I am sure he is ready to bolt. Do I have the right to detain him? How much force can I use? Do I call for cover? Do I yell for help? I start sizing him up to see what the best way to deal with this situation will be. If only

I could figure out what to do to delay his decision long enough for my partner to return so it is her problem too, not just mine.

Like an angel, she appears. It's like a cloak of darkness has been lifted as our suspect realizes now it's two against one. I am ready to grab him to put the cuffs on as I am sure we will be arresting him and I am sure the fight will be on. My partner approaches, says no one is at the house and there doesn't seem to be any signs of entry. She tells him that he is free to go.

Just like that it's over. No fight, no struggle, I didn't even get to use my new cuffs! My heart rate returns to normal and the shift is over. 99% boredom, 1% total adrenaline. I find many shifts will go the same way.

» » Can You fight? » »

Most recruits who go through Depot Division in Regina Saskatchewan hear war stories from instructors on what to expect when they get to their new posting. The reputation of what happens out of Surrey Detachment in B.C. is no exception. After all it is the largest operational RCMP Detachment in Canada in terms of resources and has a reputation of having a heavy workload.

I was the Training NCO at Surrey Detachment for a few years and tried to welcome the new members with enthusiasm. My intension was to instil a sense of adventure in their minds when they arrive. I get a telephone call from one member who just graduated out of Depot. He seemed cheerful enough over the phone and wanted to know who his trainer might be.

I quickly congratulated him on his transfer and asked him "Can you shoot? --- Can you fight?" adding in the same breath – "Then get your butt down here ASAP because we need you!". I didn't realize the person I was talking to was in the British Army before joining the RCMP. He was a big man and a good shot as well. His impact and contribution throughout the years in Surrey were appreciated.

» » Hookers sensing danger » »

When I arrive at VPD roll call for a practical shift as a reserve member, it's sort of a crap shoot. Even though the Sergeant should be aware that there is a reserve planning on attending that night, there is no real guarantee. If the team is flush with two man cars, there is no real need to put a reserve in the back seat or split a team up to accommodate the reserve member.

On this particular night, there is only one member working alone as it is his first night back in regular patrol. The group welcomes him to their team and introductions are made all around. Part of the duties of the team Sergeant is to assign patrol areas to each team. Most know them as they ride the same area and use the same call sign on every rotation. The lone member tonight is the exception, due to his first shift status. It is also a given that being the only one man car, he is going to be my mentor for the evening as well. I wonder how he will take that piece of news as he is obviously not new to seeing reserves.

Colin and I are introduced and he accepts the challenge of being my boss for the night. His smile is confusing as he grinned ear to ear after accepting the responsibility. He has the attention of the entire team and asks in a booming voice, "Can you run"? I have no idea where this is coming from, but carefully respond in the affirmative, gauging his reaction as I have no idea where this is going.

Colin then says that's good because this is my first night in patrol after five years as a dog handler and if he tells me to sick'em he expects I will do as instructed! Well, that broke the ice, and we were off to our assigned patrol area.

Early in our shift a general radio call was made to the cars in our district. One of the areas we patrol is the hooker stroll just north of Hastings around Clark Drive. It seems that one of the cars driving the stroll has a child in the back seat of the car. The car is described and as usual, we go about our business.

A few hours later, we get a call from radio. We have been assigned to a suspicious circumstances call in an industrial area. There is a car parked on the road and the person behind the wheel seems to be unresponsive. His head is at a strange angle and he is either passed out or dead. A passerby tried to see if they could help and decided it best to call the police. More alarming is the fact that there is a child in the back seat of the car crying.

We rush to the location not knowing what to expect. Upon our arrival, the scene is exactly as it was reported. After a lot of banging on the window of the car, there is no response from the driver. The child in the back seat is hysterical.

We decide that the only thing we can do is break the window to gain entry. After a quick call to the supervisor for permission, we are surprised by the driver waking and opening the door.

We take this guy and move him to the back of the cruiser where my partner is going to start his interview to find out what is going on. My partner looks at me and says "Take care of the little boy". The boy is hysterical. He is around three or four years old and has no idea what is going on.

Due to the initial call, we had called for an ambulance to attend the scene in case there was a medical issue to deal with. As in most cases, both fire and ambulance are dispatched and at that moment I hear the sirens approaching. I can see them, but the way the road is laid out, they can't see us. I take the boy from the back seat of the subject's car and tell him to come with me. We move to the front seat of the police cruiser and I reach in and hit the lights to attract the fire truck searching for us. This caused a big change in the boy as he stared at the lights flashing on the police car. Just like any little boy, he was mesmerized by the lights and had something to think of other than crying.

The night was not going to be a good one for this father. He was arrested for child endangerment, and his son was immediately taken into custody by child services at the scene. He would now have to battle the system for the right to see his son.

At this point, radio dispatch has more information for us. When arriving we had provided a description of the car and the plate. Radio confirms that this, along with the description of the man we have, all matches as being the same car reported earlier in the shift as driving the hooker stroll with a child in the rear.

Being ever so curious, I ask how we know this and the radio operator states it was a report from a couple of concerned hookers. They saw this car driving around looking for a 'date' and saw the child in the back. They had called 911 and provided the details to the operator as they were concerned for the child's safety! It just proves that even though they may not have chosen what would be considered a respectable career, they still have a good sense of right and wrong.

» » **Rough water** » »

As a junior member in a small northern Manitoba Detachment, I often had to do interesting and sometimes out of the ordinary tasks that I never learned about in Depot. One such task was when I was directed by my NCO, to escort the Judge, Crown Attorney and court party across the lake to a cultural camp they had been invited to by the local Probation Officer.

This task was not a difficult one, I knew my way around the lake, and had lots of experience on a boat (even though at the time I didn't have the boat course). I took this opportunity as a great way to get out on the water and maybe even do a little fishing if time permitted.

Our trip across the lake to the camp was, for the most part, uneventful, except for the fact that I did have a hard time finding the camp. After a few directions from a local cottage owner, we were on our way and enjoying the day at the camp. We toured the lake with some of the locals, looked at ancient rock paintings and even picked rocks on the shore with some of the kids.

We had a great lunch of fried fish, bannock, corn on the cob and tea, and then visited with the elders at the camp. I managed to slip away down to the boat where my fishing rod and tackle box were and made a few casts from shore. I was lucky enough to catch a large pike and give it to our gracious hosts.

That was when I noticed the dark bank of clouds rolling in from the north. The cloud was advancing on us quickly, and I could tell that there was a lot of rain and wind coming with them. I advised the court party to hurry, as we had 40 kilometers of water to cover, and I wasn't sure if we would get back before the storm caught us.

This is where it gets interesting. I am usually quite obsessive when it comes to the boat, especially when it involves ropes like the anchor line. I normally keep the rope stowed up in the bow where it can't get out. This time, though, I simply untied the line from the tree, bundled it in a loose ball and threw it on the floor of the boat. We all climbed into the boat and made our quick retreat south toward home. A few miles into our return trip, the storm rolled in on top of us, bringing rough swells and tons of rain. As we were pitched and tossed in the water, I noticed a large wave grab onto the loose end of the anchor line and begin pulling the rope from out of the boat. My first thought was if that goes into the prop, we are done for. I quickly killed the gas on the big outboard engine. At that exact moment, the Judge, who was seated next to me, had the same thought, and stood up to pull the rope back into the boat. When I killed the engine, he was thrown violently forward, hitting his head on the small platform in the bow of the boat, giving him a large cut on his forehead which began to bleed. My mind brought up alarming thoughts but the one that stands out was the fact that I had an upcoming trial the following month, on a large case that I had been working on, and he would be the Judge in charge of the matter. I was sure that I was going to pay for this for the remainder of my service.

Luckily for me, the Judge was good natured about the whole thing, saying maybe he shouldn't have stood up when he did. I was a rough trip back, and we even had to wait the storm out behind an island. The good news was we made it back, wet and cold, but we all were glad to get home. The Judge never held it against me as he and I still chuckle over the whole episode when we see each other.

Where is the Car?

I was fresh out of Depot Division in a small Detachment in rural Nova Scotia. It was snowing heavily and we received a 911 call of a domestic disturbance complaint. Another member and I made a patrol to the remote rural residence. As I pulled in the yard I noticed six or seven vehicles and lights on in the house. Two males approached the police car as I came to a stop. Being my first domestic, I didn't want the males to jump me in the car so I quickly got out. When I got out of the police car with the other member I was successful in calming down the two males and we all went inside the residence to investigate further. A short time later, the other member approached me and was frantic. She advised me that our police car was gone! I ran outside in disbelief and quickly radioed Telecoms and our Detachment Commander of the situation. I commandeered a pickup truck and followed the tracks in the snow, finding the police car about 300 meters down the road around a corner with fresh footprints in the snow leading back to the scene. The keys were still in the ignition, where I had left them. - I'll never do that again!!

CHAPTER #3

Memorable Drunks

» » Showing Respect » »

"There is always one or two characters that stick out and keep coming back as memorable individuals we had to deal with almost daily. One clearly sticks out as saying the same thing every time I tried to take his coat or jacket off as I was booking him in for being drunk.

He would push me aside and say "Don't touch me, I've been in the B.C. Pen,- Kill if I have to." This same individual would treat you with respect as long as you gave him some as well. I put this to the test one day when responding to a call in front of one of the local hotels.

Sure enough, this same individual was out on the street putting on a show for the public so I expected the worst. I pulled the P.C. in front of the hotel just a few steps from where my target was actively putting on a display. He knew I was coming for him and began to let the whole world know that they were about to see the biggest fight of their life. I merely opened up the right rear door to the police car, came sharply to attention and saluted this individual as he approached me. It must have taken him quite by surprise as he exchanged salutes and entered the police car without fuss. The passing public got a chuckle out of this procedure, but it got the job done.

» » Where am I? » »

Kamloops, B.C. – mid 1970's - We approached an intoxicated male just in front of the Detachment. He appeared bewildered and didn't know where he was nor where his truck was. My partner, an auxiliary member, asked him how long he'd been in Regina. Our subject disagreed he was in Regina because we were in central B.C. Upon booking him in for being drunk in a public place I discovered a gas slip he had that same date marked Boston Bar, B.C. I immediately told him I would buy his truck if he could fill up in Boston Bar B.C. and drive all the way to Regina on one tank of gas. The poor man was escorted to a cell muttering, asking himself how he was going to get back to B.C.

» » "YES DEAR" » »

I was going through the motions of collecting as much physical evidence as possible on an impaired driver I had arrested. Breathalyzers were not on the scene yet. I got this one farmer into the office and asked him to open up his wallet to count this money. He started with a 1 dollar bill. "One" he says as he continued to pull out a $5.00 bill and said "Two", and so on. I told him I thought he made a mistake and he should recount his money. He complied and did the same thing again. I felt the need to ask him to count again as he made some mistakes. To this he replied in a snide way "Yes Dear!!!"

» » Put the round key in my ignition » »

It's near midnight and I observe a station wagon leave the local pub. It's full of people and the vehicle is making excessive noise. I decide to check this vehicle and find an impaired driver behind the wheel. After dealing with him I return to the vehicle and ask the heavy-set lady in the front seat to place the keys I gave her in the ignition and start the car. I wanted to check and see if the muffler was causing the loud noise from the vehicle.

She kept trying to put the round- headed key in the ignition. As this was a Ford product I told her not to play around with the round key, but rather put the square key in. She looked at me and said "If you've got the round key - I'll put it in my ignition" and then she burst out laughing. I knew I'd been had by her innuendo so I started the car myself and decided to have the vehicle towed. The rest of the people in the car were laughing so hard I gave them a break and sent them on their way with a local cab.

» »   Place Nose Here!   » »

I can still see the mark left on the book-in counter at Vancouver Jail. It was just about 10 inches from the edge and probably was a small hole in the arborite from original installation. Someone placed, in small letters, the words "Place nose here!" which I am sure a number of members bringing in patrons could relate to.

» »   "What color is your name?   » »

Every once in a while I would try to get an arrested person confused when booking them in for being drunk. I would ask questions like: "Tell me, what colour is your name, true or false?" or – "If a light sleeper sleeps with a light on, does a hard sleeper sleep with a window open?" or – "Do I remind you of a cab with both doors open? This last question would get mixed reactions because I stood out as having very large protruding ears. For the most part humour got me further than getting individuals up tight if they got a little difficult. There were times when joking around was not appropriate, so you stuck to being serious. Once in a while you could insert a little humour and have fun with people while executing your duty.

» »   Faking Back Injury   » »

I had to deal with a character by the name of "Archie R" who was a big man with some military background. A call was received to remove him from some local establishment which was a youth hostel in Kamloops. I'd dealt with this person before, and knew that if I was too aggressive, several people would be required to subdue this man and take him into custody. I entered the premises and found Archie on the second floor landing lying on his back and in an apparent drunken stupor. Upon approaching him, he demanded that I kiss him right there and then. I knew at this moment I had my hands full so I called for backup and an ambulance. Archie was a chronic complainer of back pain and threatened on occasion to sue the police if we didn't treat him right. He lay there, stiff as a board, not wishing to cooperate with my bargaining to get him out of the building. He was a regular at the youth hostel. This man had also been dealt with by ambulance personnel in the past. They had arrived by this time and told me they had concern that he may have fallen down the stairs and reinjured his back.

Archie continued to be uncooperative. At this point I had nothing to lose. I know that sooner or later we would be struggling to contain this man, perhaps in a strait jacket, and get him to the hospital for treatment. I recalled that he had some military background and had seen a T.V. program earlier about Vietnam veterans who were having flashbacks about their careers, so I gave it a try. In a stern voice I said "Archie, who the hell is your commanding officer? - stand up while I'm talking to you." Archie immediately got up from his prone position and stood at attention, as ridged as one could stand, looked straight ahead and yelled out "SIR." I can't recall his exact words after that as I was dumbfounded that he would react that way.

I took advantage of the situation and pointed out to him that if he didn't obey orders there would be serious consequences. By this time the paramedics had arrived and were already preparing the medical stretcher for him. Archie, still standing at attention and looking straight ahead, made no move to escape from what was unfolding before him.

I told him to get down and lay down on the stretcher, as we were going to take him to the hospital for treatment. At this command he smartly stepped forward and lay on the stretcher allowing the paramedics to strap him in. He was transported to hospital for further assessment.

» » High speed Chase! » »

I was driving a drunk back to his home on the Reserve in Alberta as I did not feel he was a candidate to be placed in cells. As I was driving this subject back, he began to start a conversation with me by asking "Do you guys get many high speed chases out this way?" I replied that I did not think so because most cars on the reserve are not in good enough shape to even be in a high speed chase. My prisoner then added - 'I was in a high speed chase about a year ago, but I gave up, I got tired because I ran out of breath."

» » The Silzer Cup » »

The "Silzer CUP" – The distinction we established in honor of our Supervisor. There was competition between two different zones on the watch as to which one could pick up more drunks in one night. The north zone had more potential clients because of the area they policed. The south zone had fewer possible clients based on the patrol area. It was nip and tuck for numbers by the end of the night. One member on the south zone sensed their side was losing ground so he ventured into another jurisdiction which was the down town east side of Vancouver. The member picked up a few bringing them back to take them off the streets for being drunk. By the end of the shift the south side had won the cup and the north side wondered how this could be. Some of the drunks released the next morning wondered how they wound up in Surrey.

» » One in my Cookie! » »

I am working as a guard in a female capacity in the Surrey Detachment Cell Block area when a female prisoner is brought in. She had numerous jewelry type studs in her ears, nose and lip area and was told by my supervisor to remove all of them before she could be placed in cells. The prisoner replied "All of them?" to which she was told "Yes – all of them." The prisoner than exclaimed "I also have one in my Cookie!" – do you want that one too?" My supervisors face turned a few shades of red and in embarrassment said there was no need to do that.

»» Kangaroo Court »»

In Kamloops, B.C. during the mid-1970's we got a call to pick up a transient who was found drunk hitching a ride on a CPR train coming through town. It was late at night when we managed to remove the subject and place him in cells. One of the members thought it might be a good idea to hold court with this individual and perhaps teach him a lesson. It was about 3:00 a.m. when it was arranged to bring the subject up to court room #2 as the court rooms were all located on the top floor of the police building. One of the members happened to find a judge's robe just inside one of the court rooms and the scene was staged.

The subject was brought up to the court room and was still in some minor state of intoxication. One of the members put on the judge's robe and sat in the judge's chair to start the proceedings. The other member read the charge as one of stealing a ride from the CPR and being drunk in public. The subject was told that he would be sentenced to one day in jail or time in custody and was instructed not to come back to Regina again.

A few hours later the same members were responsible for releasing the overnight prisoners towards 6:30 a.m.AM after they had had a few hours of sleep. The subject who had been taken upstairs to the earlier court proceedings was also released and reminded once again not to come back to Regina again. This poor soul left the cell block area somewhat confused not knowing where he was at all.

»» Funniest Arrest »»

I was stationed in northern BC during the 1990's and recall arresting an individual whom I had to place in cell and to release him when sober. As I was booking this gentlemen in a cell the prisoner became verbally abusive. There were not too many Afro American RCMP members in northern B.C. at the time so the prisoner was giving me the gears about the color of my skin. He would say things like "Constable, you remind me of Bill Cosby, are you Bill Cosby? A little while later in the middle of his verbal abuse he would ask again, "You remind me of Michael Jackson, are you Michael Jackson? I replied - "If you don't shut up I will remind you of Mike Tyson!".

» » Just want to stay for the night » »

It's the middle of winter in northern Alberta. A slightly intoxicated male rings the doorbell at the office in the middle of the night. After the member opens the door, the man asks if he can be lodged in cells overnight since it is so cold and he has nowhere else to go for the night. His home is 50 kilometers away and there are no cab services. The member replies that he can't lodge him overnight as he did not do anything wrong and it was against their policy to just hold persons overnight like that. He basically turned the fellow around and shut the door on him.

Thirty minutes later, a complainant reports a stolen car. Members locate the car, get into a pursuit for nearly an hour before the suspect hits the ditch. They bring him in and guess who; it was the same man that earlier had asked to stay overnight. As he gets booked in, he makes the statement, "Can I go to jail for the night now?"

» » Arnold ZIFFLE - Green Acres! » »

I had left the RCMP for almost two years. In 1971, I was rehired and transferred to Kamloops, B.C. One of my first calls was to pick up a drunk in front of the Leland Hotel. It was midafternoon and a hot summer day. I am sure that anyone who consumed alcohol and hit the afternoon heat when they walked out of a bar would not last long without showing strong signs of impairment.

Upon arrival I could see two individuals, who appeared to be friends of the subject I was interested in, trying to help him walk down the street.

My intension was to place this fellow under arrest and put him in cells to dry out. His two friends insisted that they would take care of him and wanted to take him home. I thought it may be a good idea to let them take care of this problem. I just needed to get some information as to who the subject was so I politely asked the drunk what his name was. His two friends were still assisting him to stay on his feet. The drunk snapped back at me with the name "Arnold ZIFFLE". I wanted further clarification so I asked "Where do you live?" He again snapped back in his drunken stupor "Green Acres". I took this information down in my notebook and allowed the two close friends to take their buddy away. Case closed!.

I found out later that Arnold ZIFFLE was in fact the name given to a Pig on the T.V. show at the time called "Green Acres". I guess I had been taken to the cleaners on this one. I realized that I had not watched this program on T.V. so was not aware of this. I am sure the two friends thought I was an idiot putting the name in my notebook. It was a hard lesson learned.

» » Get her out of the car » »

My partner with only three months on the job and I were sent to a disturbance call at a home. Upon arriving we noticed an older lady (70+) in the front seat of a large car in the driveway. She was banging on the passenger window as we approached. At the same time a gentlemen and another lady came out of the house and seemed panicky.

They were saying how happy they were to see us and hopefully we could help them get Gladys out of the car. They were upset because Gladys was locked in the car. They were telling me that the doors were locked and she couldn't get them unlocked. I looked at my partner who was trying all the doors on the car. He was trying to explain to Gladys how to push the automatic door lock button but she didn't understand. He was able to open the back driver's side door and reached into to the front and unlocked the front door so Gladys could get out. Once out of the car, Gladys gave my partner a big hug and we left shaking our heads. You just know alcohol was involved in this case.

CHAPTER #4

Driving Incidents

» » Poor road conditions » »

It's mid-winter and on the way to the airport of this small northern community, I notice a red Dept. of Transport truck in the ditch with two sets of footprints in the snow coming back to the road. I meet the supervisor at the airport some time later and determine he was the driver of the truck. When I asked him what happened he replied, "While driving out towards the airport last night, I had one hand on her hind end and - the other one I completely forgot about". This man was too honest, so I wrote the incident off in my report as poor road conditions.

» » Getting there fast » »

A Member on patrol enters an intersection and is met by an impaired driver who hits the patrol car almost broadside. There are no injuries and as the member gets out of his patrol car to approach the driver of this car, the guy rolls down his window and states "Boy, you guys sure got here fast!!"

» » My dog was raped » »

Just out of Houston, B.C. a member on highway patrol stops a car for speeding. The only occupants in the car were the driver and his dog. When asked why he was speeding the driver responded "My dog was just raped and I'm taking her to the vet." The ticket was still issued.

» » I was not driving » »

A prohibited driver was being booked into Surrey Cells in preparation for an early morning court appearance. Upon being booked in, the subject kept telling the member: "I wasn't driving, I was only backing up!"

» » Topless Skidoo » »

My biggest problem in driving a police transport was not watching when I was backing up. I was on duty at Fort Chipewyan Detachment and got a call regarding some sort of disturbance at the local restaurant in the middle of the afternoon. I quickly jumped into our 4X4 Dodge suburban police transport and backed out of the driveway in front of the Detachment to head downtown. I had forgotten that the local bush pilot had just pulled up behind the suburban with his private skidoo to come and see the Cpl.

The suburban had no rear windows and the rear view mirrors did not pick up the image of a skidoo parked behind me. While backing up in haste, I remember feeling a lot of crunching and rumbling going on. Out from the front of the P.C. appeared a vision of a skidoo with the top half being completely shaved off and damaged to the point of not being operational. I had backed over the whole unit. Needless to say a full report had to be submitted to Sub Division, with the Force paying out a large amount of funds to repair this man's skidoo. When the Sub Division NCO saw me on my next trip into Edmonton, he remarked that he was going to requisition the Force to issue me a Dog Team, as this form of transportation only knew how to go forwards and it would save the Force a lot of money.

» » True to the end » »

I knew a member who was working in Ontario and was the victim of a police car accident where, in a strange set of circumstances, a pair of Canada Geese flying low and close together flew right into the path of the front of the police transport. They did not survive the impact. After completing his notes related to the damage to his police transport, he made the comment that he felt both flew into the police transport as if they were in the process of committing suicide as a couple.

CHAPTER #5

That close call

»» **Fatal MVA** »»

Every member has some memory that he or she would sooner forget than think about. It is not that easy because every once in a while you relive that same scene all over again and ask yourself "Why was I picked to survive that ordeal?" This is one of those memories:

It's the end of September 1966 and I'm only about three weeks out of training. The Corporal I'm stationed with decides to go out into the country and follow up on a complaint of a cow being shot on a side road. This is a rural farming area near Viking, Alberta. We are on patrol to meet an elderly retired farmer and his wife at their farm which is nestled in the rolling countryside. We were greeted at the farm home with an invite for a cup of coffee. I was exposed for the first time to not just getting the facts from a complainant but learned there was a need to just visit for a short while. My Corporal thanked the homemaker for her invite to coffee and snacks. We left the home as the elderly farmer told his wife we would only be a short while and he would be back. Little did she know this would be the last time she saw him alive and well.

The three of us made a patrol down the country road not far from his farmyard until we reached a dip where our complainant had discovered one of his cows in the ditch. Upon closer examination, it was discovered that the cow was struck by some passing motorist and a piece of chrome became lodged in the side of the neck of the animal. The cow bled to death. The farmer was at least pleased to have us take the time on a Friday afternoon to examine the scene. He hoped that we might find an offending vehicle with damage consistent with the incident. From here, fate played its part in allowing me to live on to write about this incident.

It was a nice Fall afternoon with some Fall colors were beginning to show on the leaves. The air was cool and from a distance I could hear the sound of a truck rumbling down the road towards us. We had the police transport parked on the top of the hill just behind us. We had learned later that this route was being used heavily during the week by a crew spreading gravel on the back roads in the area. I observed a gravel truck come over the crest of the hill leaving a huge cloud of dust that just lingered in the quiet Fall air. His speed appeared excessive for this narrow country road. The truck blew past us in a flash as we stood on the side of the road. Just behind this gravel truck came an empty 'low bed' tractor trailer unit which had been used to haul heavy equipment. The driver of this vehicle later explained that all he saw was the break lights on the gravel truck in front of him in the cloud of dust and a police car parked at the top of the next hill. He assumed there must have been some kind of an accident on the roadway in front of him and immediately applied all breaks causing his complete unit to fishtail sideways as it was coming down the road towards us. As soon as this driver saw us, he tried to direct his unit into the ditch on the other side.

At this instant I can vividly recall reacting only to my own survival instincts and to get the hell out of the way. I can still see the Cpl. and myself throwing ourselves sideways into the ditch full of willows, water etc. Upon landing in the ditch, my quick glance back saw the back end wheels of the low bed unit just missing me by about 6 feet. It disappeared somewhere in the cloud of dust. I had lost sight of the old man that only seconds before, stood beside me at the edge of the road. If I had only grabbed him as well, perhaps things would have been different. I knew things would not look good as I got up from the partially water filled ditch.

I brushed my brown serge uniform from minor debris and found the old man lying in a prone position on the side of the road not far from where we were standing. He was in obvious pain. He had been hit by the rear end of this low bed unit, was conscious but in shock and severe pain. I looked about and as the dust settled I could see the entire low bed truck unit jackknifed and partially submerged in the slough on the opposite side of the road. All was quiet now, except for the cries of pain and moaning the old man was exhibiting as we got our thoughts collected. Somewhere in the following moments we radioed for an ambulance and tried to keep the old man comfortable. He told me he had to pee so I assisted in opening his pants and noticed blood in his urine. I knew this would not be good.

The incident was all over, but the quietness of the moment meant that help could not come quick enough. The image of those few seconds had forever been burned in my memory. In those few seconds time almost stood still and seemed like an eternity. Many thoughts passed through my mind. There was confusion on what to do next. It was so quiet. The serenity of this nice Fall scene had changed dramatically. I recall thinking to myself, as I knelt beside the injured old man, - "Great - we just told his wife we wouldn't be gone too long, and now I would have to go back to the farm and ask this women to accompany us to the hospital". I also thought to myself, this day could have been a day my retired parents in Saskatchewan could have received a Next of Kin Notification, if I had been killed. I was that close to meeting my maker.

My Corporal told me to gather up some larger stones from the gravel at the edge of the roadway and place them beside the right rear tire of the police transport. I guess he knew this would be necessary for marking just where the police transport was parked on the top of the hill, in the event a coroner's inquest was held.

The ambulance finally arrived taking the seriously injured farmer to hospital. The victim's wife was informed of the accident and arrangements were made to transport her back into town. I drove up to the hospital to deliver a few more personal belongings of this man and will never forget the sound of his anguish and cries of pain in the emergency area. The old man died of internal injuries hours later in hospital. The next day my Corporal and I conducted accident scene measurements to file the necessary fatal accident reports.

The Coroner's inquest that followed created a fair bit of controversy as to actions taken by the Mounted Police. The issue argued was whether we were protecting the area we were investigating sufficiently to alert passer-by motorists. Hind sight is always 20-20. The Coroner's Jury suggested a few recommendations but came up with a statement that this accident was a result of a set of circumstances that put no criminal blame on any parties.

I know that whenever my thoughts go back to that day, I keep thinking about that retired farmer, who I'm sure would have enjoyed a few more years looking after his cattle. If only we had met him a 1/2 hour sooner or maybe later that day.

» » Vest saves life » »

As anyone who has spent any time in Alberta knows, weather there can change as quickly as it did one night while working my shift on freeway patrol in central Alberta. I had just arrived at my residence and sat down to supper when I received a call to respond to an incident on the freeway. It was the middle of January. As I started to drive to the scene, it was "raining" and with the temperature being just right for freezing as soon as it hit the pavement.

What we had was a skating rink on the highway. I made my way to the scene, I should have just put my skates on and skated there. It would have been faster.

I parked the PC part way in the ditch and as the highway was too treacherous, I advised the people at the scene that I would take them into town. I reached into my car and that is when another vehicle crashed into my PC, driving the driver's door post into my ribs. I sustained numerous injuries, including broken ribs, collapsed lung, knee and back injury, dislocated shoulder and numerous bumps and bruises.

In the emergency room the nurse asked me to remove my storm coat. I was in excruciating pain and could not move. I told her to cut it off. She refused as she didn't want to damage "government property". I told her, in my best English, through clenched teeth, to cut the F**king thing off. She still refused and the examination could not continue. Finally a member came in and I quickly told him that the nurse would not cut the storm coat. The member had no hesitation and grabbed a pair of scissors and much to the dismay of the nurse, shredded the coat.

After the examination, the doctor advised me that the only reason I was still breathing was because of the bullet proof vest I had on at the time of the accident. The vest had cushioned and spread out the blow from the door post. This caused more ribs to be broken and my lung to collapse. The alternative would have been less broken ribs, but they would have been driven through my lungs and shattered them and I wouldn't be here today. The vest had saved my life.

» » **What if I pushed you?** » »

My first posting was to Prince Rupert rural detachment. Part of my duties was to respond to complaints at the fish canneries on the Skeena River, that were about 5 miles out of town. One night I got called out from home by the city dispatcher. Someone was complaining about a noisy party at one of the cabins. These cabins were lived in by locals that worked at the canneries during fishing season. The cabins were built on the bank of the river on stilts over the water. They had a board walk on the water side of the cabin that was about 10 feet in the air, then down to a rocky river bank. I drove out to the cannery and located the noisy party. I entered the cabin and spoke to the occupants. After some discussion with the group of 6 young males 16 to 19 years old, I convinced them to close the party down. We all filed out onto the boardwalk. One individual walked up to me and asked what I was going to do if he pushed me off the boardwalk? I looked down over the edge onto the rocks, then said "I don't know, but we are both going to get hurt!" He looked at the rocks, and then at me, and said "yes - you could be right". With that, they all turned and went home.

» » Chasing a Mustang » »

It was my first week on the job and my trainer and I were going to stop a red Mustang that was flying down the highway. My trainer was driving. The Mustang wouldn't stop. We ended up calling it in to telecoms and advising them we were in a high speed near this small northern community. We followed the vehicle around the reserve, speeding excessively. We ended up getting the suspect's vehicle to jump over a concrete divider at the Native school ground, which slowed him down. Our suspect was nose to nose with the police truck. He put the Mustang into drive and rammed us head on. Thank God the airbags did not deploy.

This wrecked his car and luckily, my trainer was able to get the driver out of the vehicle while I was able to get the passenger out of the vehicle. After four years of service, I have never been as scared on the job as I was that day. I couldn't make any notes, my hands were shaking so badly. Unfortunately, the guy laid a public complaint of excessive force against my trainer and my trainer was charged criminally with assault. This charge was eventually dropped in court.

» » Man with a rifle » »

I responded to a call at Wood Mountain Saskatchewan where we were informed a drunk male was wandering through the sparsely populated neighbourhood shooting at random with a high powered rifle. Those living in the immediate area were very concerned for their safety. My partner and I rushed out to the area with little back up as in those days the Emergency Response Teams (ERT), were non-existent.

On reflecting back, I recall approaching an area where witnesses saw the suspect enter a heavily wooded bush area. Our intension was to try and locate the general area where the suspect was. There, by the grace of

God, we went and luckily found the drunk passed out in the bush with his rifle at the ready.

We could have been sitting ducks and our wives would have received next of kin notification had this individual decided to use us for target practice. My thoughts go towards members today who still put themselves at risk in daily situations where firearms might be available and in possession of deranged people.

»» This never happened! »»

High Speed pursuits are a front page article or hit the news on a daily basis. This one high speed pursuit in Saskatchewan had the Force Aircraft involved where a suspect vehicle had been followed for some time. As the pursuit continued the pilot saw an opportunity to try a new tactic. He proceeded to land his plane on the highway in such a fashion causing the suspect vehicle to veer off the highway and lose control. The suspect hit the ditch and the chase was over. The pilot of the Force Aircraft approached the investigating pursuit member and made the following statement. "This never happened!", as he was quite concerned his actions were against the aeronautics rules and would put his career in jeopardy. The media never heard a thing about the incident.

»» Dodging the bullet »»

I was working as a Washington State Trooper several years ago and had a traffic stop for a speeding violation on the I- 5 Freeway south of Seattle. The violator was going 30 mph over the speed limit. I approached the driver and in a smooth way wanted clarification as to his reason for speeding. The subject I checked replied that he was not watching.

I verified his identification and he did not come across our police data system as a person of interest. I paused for a second and approached the driver with this response. "I'll tell you what I'm going to do. I will write you up for speeding but not for 30 mph over, - just 20 mph over the speed limit, can you live with this?" The violator accepted this process and took the ticket.

Three and a half hours later, my supervisor from head office queried me about a ticket I had written out to a subject earlier on the I-5 highway near Seattle, Washington for speeding 20 mph over the limit. They had found the ticket I wrote out in his vehicle. I confirmed this matter and was told by my supervisor that this subject shot and killed a State Trooper in the State of Oregon who was rude to him while stopping him for speeding. Apparently this fellow was sitting on his .38 caliber revolver when I picked him up for speeding near Seattle, Washington. Good manners pay off is the moral of this story.

» »   **Wrong gender**   » »

A female member of the RCMP did a routine stop of a violator for speeding in Saskatchewan. She went about her check as she has done so many times checking for driver's license and registration etc. While she was doing her check through the Dispatch she was not aware her suspect was in fact an escape from the nearby Bowden Correctional Centre. After approaching the driver and issuing him her citation, the driver handed over his revolver and made the following statement to her. "If you had been a male, I would have shot you!"

» »   **Lucky Friday Bank Shooting**   » »

Friday February 2nd, 1990 seems like only yesterday.

My wife and I got up and headed out to a credit union in Richmond, B.C. to cash a $6,000.00 cheque which had just been presented to us by a relative whose finances were very questionable.

After some discussion with the credit union we were presented with the cash. After stopping for breakfast we headed for the CIBC at 54th & Victoria Drive in Vancouver.

It was just after ten in the morning and I was surprised to see how busy it was in that area. I had to park about a block away and encouraged my wife to wait in the car but she insisted in going into the bank with me.

All the tellers were busy and in fact there was a line up around the usual ropes and posts. I recall nudging my wife, who was ahead of me, telling her to recount the cash, which we were about to deposit. She said she would not do so because there might be a bank robber in the bank. Little did we know that he actually was the man directly behind us.

We reached the middle teller and I handed the cash to her. She counted the bills then straightened them up and then put them into a money counting machine to again count them. I am not a very patient person when it comes to simple things, like counting money and was somewhat annoyed at the length of time this simple transaction took. When the teller took the bills from the machine she bundled them and placed an elastic band around them.

Suddenly she threw the bundle of bills onto the floor under the counter and looked to her left, my right.

I looked to my right and standing in front of the teller to my right was a bank robber. He was about my age 55 years, and far too old to be robbing banks, I thought. He was standing with his back to the teller, a revolver in his right hand and some cash in his left hand. He held the revolver in a level position pointing it in a menacing manner at the crowd of now terrified bank customers. He did not say a word.

I had been a Vancouver City police constable from 1956 to 1965 when the internal police politics made me quit, and still, my police mentality kicked in. I quickly moved towards the robber and grasped the wrist of the right hand that was holding the revolver and pushed it upwards towards the ceiling. I did not want to force it downwards or left or right for fear of the bullet hitting an innocent person.

Unfortunately, the revolver discharged at the point when it was level and pointing directly at my throat area and only about a foot away from me.

The impact spun me around and lifted me off the floor. I landed on my back with my feet facing the front doors of the bank. There was no pain whatsoever. I said to my wife, who was bending over me, "Have I been shot?" She replied, "Yes". She was very calm and collected and checked me over. There was no bullet exit wound and there was only a small drop of blood on the Leo medallion that I wore on a chain around my neck. I took off my watch and ring and necklace and gave it to my wife as I had been to emergency before, then I propped my head up with my hands so I could watch the ongoing action.

In the meantime, the bandit had headed for the front door to escape. The stolen money was spread over the bank floor and now he wanted to save his own hide. Unfortunately a retired VPD (Vancouver Police Department) officer who had never ever faced an armed man during his career was also in the bank and he jumped the bandit. The struggle was on the bank floor about half ways to the front door. The remainder of the bank customers were standing well back obviously quite shaken by the events. The retired VPD officer, William Murray Nicol, 65 years old, was having difficulty restraining the bandit. Unbeknown to everyone at this point the bandit was Peter Zivkovic, age 49 years, an escaped convict from an Alberta prison where he had been pumping iron. Nevertheless, Nicol managed to get the revolver away from the bandit and slide it across the floor, out of reach.

Next, another bank customer, George Albert Porter, a senior 75 year old retired military man, jumped on top of the struggling pair. Porter placed a toehold on the bandit and when that did not work he used a double toehold and the bandit was secured. The bandit was complaining, "You're hurting me". My wife nicknamed us "The Geritol Team".

The Vancouver City Police arrived with guns drawn thus firmly securing the scene. The bandit was whisked away in the wagon and I was taken by ambulance to the Vancouver General Hospital. (VGH).

At VGH, it was determined that I was very lucky. The bullet had fractionally missed my windpipe and all of my bones. The bullet was lodged in my upper shoulder area on my back.

Three days later on Monday, the doctor came into my hospital room and removed the bullet, handing it to a VPD detective who was standing nearby.

I persuaded the doctor to immediately release me and the detective drove me home. I learned that the internal VPD politics were no different now; only the names of the players had changed. There was physical pain now but it was no different in the hospital then at home. There is no place like home.

There was of course a preliminary hearing, followed by a trial date being set. Initially the accused plead not guilty to the numerous charges, which included attempted murder. In subsequent plea-bargaining he plead guilty to a reduced charge of aggravated assault, bank robbery and some other sundry charges. He was sentenced to 2 more life sentences and is now at Kent prison in Agassiz.

In the days after the shooting phone calls, cards, and letters arrived, even a letter from the then prime minister, Jean Chretien. The surprising culmination was the awarding of the Medal of Bravery on June 18, 1993 to all three participants who now have the initials "M.B." after their name.

PS: After the court hearing and the lapse of the appeal period I went to the VPD crime laboratory and was given the actual .38 caliber bullet that had penetrated my body as well as the casing. I took them to a jeweler and he joined them together and drilled a hole in the casing so that I could wear it on my neck chain. I wear it all the time and it reminds me how very lucky I am to be alive. Russell D. Reid, M.B. (former Vancouver PC 567).

CHAPTER #6

Partners I Remember

»» Hot in uniform »»

It was mid-July in 1973 and we were instructed to wear boots and breaches, long sleeve shirts and Stetsons. It was a Centennial Year and the Mounted Police were expected to look like part of the Canadian Heritage. Needless to say it was some uncomfortable patrolling in police vehicles that had no air conditioning. My partner, Steve, a seasoned traffic officer and I were called to a minor motor vehicle accident in the downtown core of Kamloops, B.C. It was so hot out there, 95 -100 degrees. The local radio station was asking people to try and fry an egg on the sidewalk and report their findings. I recall seeing perspiration running down the nose of my partner as he was trying to look as professional as possible. The driver of the car, an elderly lady, remarked that in such warm weather it must be tough to work in uncomfortable uniforms. My partner replied "It wouldn't be so bad ma'am, if we didn't have to wear long johns." The look on this lady's face was priceless.

»» Get your head read »»

One specific N.C.O., a sergeant who worked with me at the front counter of Edmonton rural Detachment in 1966, made an impression on me. He was confronted by a complainant who was making all kinds of demands. I listened to the conversation in hopes of learning how he would handle this person. Words became quite heated over the counter when the complainant, a middle aged women, dressed in business attire stated "Do you know who I am; I could make this very difficult for you etc.etc?" To all this the N.C.O. replied "Do you know who I am, I'm Christopher Columbus and I've discovered that you're nothing but a pain in the ass, so I want you to get out of here, get your head read and then come back and see me!".

The complainant left in a huff. I thought to myself "Wow" that is an unusual way of dealing with a complainant.

»» Stationary patrol »»

Nothing could be more boring than to do a stationary patrol. That's where you park your police car in such a manner as to leave the perception that you are monitoring traffic etc. It just so happened that a colleague of mine took the opportunity to park the P.C., roll the window down far enough to place the Stetson hat brim in such a position so that the window would grab a hold of it. Than he would slump into a comfortable position leaving his head just underneath the Stetson hat and go immediately into catnapping. The passing public never knew any different.

»» Identity crises »»

I worked with a Supervisor, whose name was Silzer. He took it upon himself to issue his name tag to a number of key members on his watch (the ones he probably thought would cause him some difficulty with complaints against members by the end of the night). If anyone came forward with a complaint against Cst. Silzer, he would quickly reply that he could not do the internal investigation because his name was implicated in the complaint. It appeared he employed a good management practice to pass the buck.

»» Taking another approach »»

We had received a complaint of a man who was burning a tire and other debris in his back yard. The neighbours were complaining about the smoke and the fire and wanted this man to quit what he was doing. The fire department showed up and quickly put it out. They noticed the man was a difficult individual to deal with as he felt he had a right to burn whatever he wanted. When we arrived to find out what was happening, it was learned that this man wanted to have a little fire in his back yard and couldn't find anything around his yard that would burn well so he cut up an old tire and set it on fire. His neighbours complained. The man was quite belligerent towards us and showed minor signs of being under the influence of alcohol.

We had our hands tied in terms of what we could do as this man was on his own property. The fire department had already put out the fire. While the man continued to be belligerent, my partner approached him and advised him that he was the lowest form of life on the earth. My partner's additional comments towards the man surely got him a little hot under the collar. As my partner left the yard this man continued to follow behind with his own arguments. As he left his yard and walked towards the police car he was now located in a public place. He was promptly placed under arrest for being drunk in public and the problem was solved. It was obvious my partner had taken an innovative approach into luring this man into a public area where our authority could kick in and solve the problem.

» » **A shitty experience** » »

During another unfortunate sexual assault/forcible confinement investigation whilst assigned to the Vernon Detachment GIS, my partner and I myself were required to work overtime throughout the entire night after a regular 14:00-02:00 hr shift. The investigation led us out into the backwoods in the Lumby detachment area where a suspect with biker connections resided. Well into the next morning we arrested the suspect without incident and the accused led us out to the alleged scene of the crime. He was quite proud of his accomplishment and gave a defence that the act had been done with the alleged victim's consent.

That night was a very long and intense night and we both consumed a tremendous amount of coffee in order to keep alert and focused. In any event, during the brief stop at the scene in a rural farm area, I suddenly felt extreme and violent stomach cramps thus indicating an immediate desire and need to purge any and all bodily substances. I immediately instructed my trusty partner to lift the rear trunk of the unmarked police cruiser in order to ensure privacy and block the view from the accused who was still seated in the back seat.

Within seconds, I quickly made my move into the nearby ditch and the dastardly deed was carried out. With a smile of relief on my face, it suddenly occurred to me that it was time to clear up the necessary paperwork. Something I learned long ago in Depot training I guess – The job isn't complete until the paperwork is completed. With the threat of oncoming traffic and a partner who somehow found humour in this situation, I called upon my so called friend/partner to make good and search out the police cruiser for some tissue or similar artefact. Be damned, there was not one shred of a cloth, report paper or a book to enable completion of the task at hand. To my amusement and possibly disbelief, it occurred to me that my "shorts" may just suit this need to perfection. You guessed it, "Rip", "Rip", "Rip"- and off came the knickers and to my amazement, the job was complete.

I knew at that very moment, that this little private matter would no doubt return to haunt me in the future. You guessed it. That little private matter turned up again while being transferred from Vernon Detachment. Yup, while my wife and I were being honoured in front of approximately two hundred guests at the transfer party, my NCO proudly shared this little story for all to enjoy. In fact, they made mention of having sent out a police service dog team who made a positive location of the alleged evidence involved. I was presented with a pair of well soiled underwear which of course made the wife and me very proud of my accomplishment.

» » Self Absorbed » »

"Bill was in love with himself – narcissistic to the max. He loved looking at himself in the mirror, flexing his muscles, and especially loved the sound of his own voice. Bill was stationed at a small detachment in B.C. when he was a rookie cop, fresh out of Depot. This Detachment provided 24 hour service to the community, but in the wee hours of the morning, between 03:00 and 07:00 a.m, there was just one member on shift. One morning, around 05:30 a.m., Bill was in the detachment killing time for that last hour before the day shift arrived. He turned on the intercom system within the office and pretended he was an airline pilot. "Ladies and gentlemen, this is your captain speaking. Our flight time today will be 4 hours and 15 minutes and we'll be flying at an altitude of 35 thousand feet with a cruising speed of 400 mph. The weather in Honolulu is a balmy 21 degrees under … yada, yada, yada. Unbeknown to Bill, a day shift member had come in early that morning to work out in the weight room and overheard Bill doing his thing over the intercom. Bill was teased after this about which flight he was on.

On another morning, again, during the wee hours of his shift, Bill was on shift and once again alone. This time he was in the bathroom practicing his "Quick Draw" in front of the mirror. You guessed it, he shot the mirror out that morning, and totally shattered that handsome image staring back at him.

» » **Listen Up!** » »

"I was training a new member and had to make sure that this member does not make some of the same mistakes I made in my career so far. Around the three month mark, my new recruit was starting to get a little more confident and was the type that would show signs of resenting some of the direction I was giving her. At first I was not recognizing this but then I finally decided it was time to back off and let her sink or swim and review the situation after. Our problem was solved in a different way because of a noise complaint. We were sent to a park where it was pointed out that kids were yelling and there was loud music. My partner was driving and drove through the park until we found the kids. As we approached they scattered like rats and we could see they had been drinking. They smashed their bottles and ran off into the bush and neighbouring yards. As we got out of the police car I felt it rock backwards and recalled telling her to put it in park. She snapped back "It's in Park", and both of us started off after our suspects.

I cornered one 15 year old and spoke to him. He was having a back yard party which progressed into the park. I told him to get one of his parents in order to show the parent the mess that was made by their kid and his friends.

My partner was checking out all the broken glass and came up to me. She put her face about 4 inches from mine and whispered "Where's the car going?". I looked over to see our police car going backwards at about 5 mph with all its lights on. It was about 100 yards away by now. I told my recruit to get it and off she went. At this point the parents of the 15 year old came out the back gate of their yard to watch the action. The car was heading for a ball diamond backstop and slowly turning. My partner finally caught up to the car as it just missed the backstop and was heading for a fence of a nearby yard. She opened the door to the PC and ran alongside it for a few meters before throwing herself in. She stopped the car about 10 yards before it would have gone through a private backyard fence. She brought the car back and never questioned me on directions or instructions I gave her again.

» » Dealing with Grief » »

This is one members response, after the death of four of his comrades in Mayerthorpe Alta in 2005, His message was sent through the median of the intranet communication system within the RCMP.

Things I feel that I must say in the light of the recent assassination of four of my brothers. First I must state that these are my personal views and are not necessarily the views of the RCMP or any governments I serve. Before I start I would like to qualify myself, my background and training. I have been a very proud member of the RCMP for the past 15 years serving in rural Alberta. Prior to my full time engagement in the force I served as an auxiliary member of the RCMP for 7 years in 2 detachments in B.C.

I am an experienced and senior member of this force. My duties over and above general investigations and law enforcement include providing ongoing firearms and use of force options training to members of this force.

We all deal with grief and loss differently, and as such I suppose this is the reason I feel I must write this. Throughout my career I have often wanted to write letters to the editor frustrated with our justice system or inaccurate details published by the media. On many occasions we as a police force have been unfairly criticized based on partial truths and limited facts presented by the media or persons of less desirable qualities. We as police officers quietly and professionally accept this as we are restricted by civil and criminal liabilities, privacy laws, policies, and the potential of hampering good investigations to reveal all the facts to the Canadian public. If the citizens of this great country were provided with all the situational factors when officers were criticized I'm confident they would support decisions and actions taken.

The loss of the 4 members last week is gut wrenchingly sad and a gigantic loss that has produced unbearable grief. This loss meant many things to many people but it definitely was not a surprise. The citizens of this great country have no idea what police deal with every day and night, no idea at all. On an average day we receive at least two e-mails warning of people who are dangerous to police for various reasons. Many are known to carry knives or guns and are eager to use them if confronted by police. Unfortunately, with what the Canadian Charter of Rights and Freedoms has turned into, we are limited in what we can do to proactively address the risk. In most of these cases we are unable to act until something bad happens leaving the public and police officers vulnerable. Police officers deal with violence more often than most people realize and are in fact put in very dangerous situations several times a day. Considering this, injury and death of our members is an expected occurrence. Unlike a soldier we often don't know who the enemy is.

In the near future we will see the media questioning and criticizing police action and policy over this situation. It is very easy when one looks back on a situation to provide a course of action to alter an outcome. Before the bashing starts I would like to state these facts in expectation of the areas of criticism that I foresee.

First of all, unlike large municipal police forces, we have very limited manpower to police vast areas. In most cases we work alone and are forced into situations with little or no back up. The limited resources we have are based on our provincial contract. Despite our efforts to increase our numbers the province has not provided more members and money requiring us to work with numbers allocated in the late 1980's. Despite population growth and crime rates, I think we continue to provide an excellent service and have done a damn fine job. It would have been nice to have placed 10 or more members on that farm crime scene to watch over things however those resources and costs are not available to us. The fact that they had two members there shows due diligence to the situation as many times I have guarded crime scenes by myself.

I suspect that the fact of the members' service level, experience and training will come under attack. I would like to say right now that if someone has the intention and planning to kill a police officer they will most certainly succeed. These 4 members were assassinated and provided with no warning or opportunity to react. Why would we place a junior member at a crime scene? How else does someone learning any trade or occupation gain experience and develop skills without exposure? As far as training goes I am proud to advise that the Mounted Police has one of the finest training facilities and curriculum in the world. Our training produces police officers of the highest caliber. If this was not the case we would not be in such high demand by the United Nations. We are continually called upon for peace keeping efforts and to rebuild and train police forces around the world.

As for national pride it should be known the Royal Canadian Mounted Police is the only police force in the world that polices at the municipal, provincial, national and international levels. That has to say something about our training and capabilities. Police officer safety is paramount in our training and recertification.

I further suspect that our justice system and Charter of Rights and freedoms will come under attack, or at least debate as it most certainly should. I would like to state that I am as are my colleagues a strong supporter of our Charter as it guarantees our freedom within this wonderful nation. I further believe that the intent of this charter was based on solid Canadian beliefs and wholesome values.

Having said that, I further believe that legal defense sector has created a billion dollar business around cutting it up and making loop holes. I do not feel the present day accepted legal interpretations were intended when it was drafted. It is ironic that the very law that was created to protect freedoms as citizens has chained and handcuffed us. It has forced us without recourse to be victims of criminals and non productive members of our society. I would suggest that common sense, fairness, reasonable and probable grounds are traits God has granted to most Canadians however withheld from some of our political leaders and our law interpreters, This allows the Supreme Court of Canada the power to veto proposed laws based on charter or constitution interpretation, limits our elected officials' power for change. This in turn makes our democratic elections very superficial which is a frightening consideration.

I heard the father of one of the deceased Mounties say "something good will come of this loss." I have been able to see two good things. I have seen the Canadian people rally around their police forces with heartfelt condolences, warm acknowledgments and appreciation for the work we do. For this we thank you. Your thoughts, prayers and kind gestures touched the hearts of everyone in our extended family. The second is that Canadians are looking at our justice system, and I believe they want change. If positive change is made and lives are saved because of it, then these deaths have not been completely without cause.

In closing I wish to say, despite what the media or any appointed committees disclose about this occurrence please remember what I have written. There was no fault with the members, policy or the RCMP. The only thing that may have changed this outcome would have been empowerment of police officers to effectively and proactively address this type of risk. The badly needed increased money and manpower may have influenced this, but likely not as the killer was focused and determined on his actions.

If you feel change is needed, real change to our Justice System I urge you do something about it. Flex your democratic muscle and force democratic change. As police officers we know who the drug dealers, rapists and psychopaths are, but we need the tools to deal with them. The same law that defines their actions as illegal also prevents their actions from being stopped or them being punished. We must put proper deterrents in our court system ensuring the message of poor behavior is not acceptable. This is our country, and I feel we must provide our police with the power to protect people again. We as citizens must also have the confidence that our police officers will not abuse this power.

If you feel change is not necessary don't feel obligated to do anything. Your police officers will continue to proudly serve Canadians in the professional way we always have but please understand the limitations restricting us. Most of all, please when the next police officer dies, don't say it was a surprise.

For those of you who read this whole letter, thank you for letting me vent and grieve in this way. Please feel free to pass this on if you feel it has any merit, if not hit delete."

Cst. Steve Smith - Cold Lake Det.

CHAPTER #7

Courtroom Memories

»» Waiting for my Organ »»

It is Wednesday afternoon in Kamloops, B.C. In the courtroom are three law school buddies. One is the judge, the other represents the Crown and the third is a defence lawyer. There is a relaxed atmosphere in the courtroom as I get ready to have the court declared open. These three colleges exchange law school memories in an informal manner for a moment. Then it's down to business and the court is opened. The first case was mine which was a simple impaired driving situation which had occurred months ago in a small parking lot near a church. My key witness was the Minister of this church. He showed up and looked his part as a man of the cloth. The Crown prosecutor made his opening remarks and asked the witness to tell his story. "I was standing in my church", the Minister stated, "It was about 5 pm and I was waiting for my organ to arrive".

At this time the judge perked up and remarked "You were waiting for WHAT?". The witness repeated the same statement in his opening remark. At this point all three members of the Bar in the courtroom started laughing and could not keep their composure. I sensed the three had some thoughts of some possible deviant behaviour taking place. The judge called for an immediate 5 minute recess and left the courtroom. He returned and apologized for the behaviour of his colleges and the case continued. The accused was eventually convicted of the offence of impaired driving.

» »   Getting innovative   » »

There have been times when after 6 months I have had to identify an accused and couldn't recall what the individual looked like. We had no picture of him on file. He could have been one of the fellows I thought was in the lobby of the courthouse but I was not sure. I knew that in this particular case I was in a bind because my partner was not sure either. It was time to be a little innovative, so I called the sheriff's office downstairs and had them page the accused to advise him there was a phone call for him. Sure enough our subject responded and gave me the advantage of recalling the man I had dealt with 6 months ago. I suffered for it on the stand later as the defence lawyer caught on to what I was trying to do, however he couldn't prove that I had instigated the call procedure in the first place. I was lucky he didn't come right out and ask me if I made that call to the Sheriff's Dept. to determine who his client really was.

» »   Parking Issue   » »

Kamloops Detachment had a very bad parking problem. The courtrooms were in the upper part of the police office. The Judge and the Officer in Charge had their own parking spots marked just outside the front door of the police office. I was working front counter one day and saw Judge Stuart Vanmale come downstairs with a determined look on his face. He approached the man I was dealing with and touched him on the shoulder remarking "Are you Judge Vanmale?" The man replied "No."- The Judge than came down with a heavy voice of authority "Of course you're not, I am, so get your goddamed car out of my parking spot". The poor man complied and moved his vehicle. Needless to say the rest of this judge's day would have been fun to watch in Court.

» »   Recruits giving testimony   » »

Setting up mock courtroom experience for recruits in training at Depot Division in Regina was a blast. As a past Depot Div. Operational Training instructor I have noted a few remarks made by various recruits who were being put through mock trial and evidence presentation training. Listed below is a sampling of some that come to mind with some explanation:

- Female member giving evidence on an impaired case - "Your honour, I found the accused laying down in the front seat of the car and the motor was still running. I opened the door, switched the car off, crawled into the car and tried to arouse him."

- A male member, who had dealt with an individual who resisted arrest, and gave the arresting member a rough time, explained "Your honour, the guy was giving me a hard time so I tried to??", (He hesitated for a second and couldn't remember to say 'subdue' and finished by saying "So I relaxed him." What in fact happened during the training scenario was quite different; He admitted on the stand that he had to use a choke hold on the accused to gain control of him.

» » **I just play the game!** » »

A young Special Constable in training took the stand in mock court and showed a lot of confidence in his presentation of evidence. As the lead instructor for this class, I took particular interest in the way he was introducing himself, "I'm Special Cst. Larat etc." I acted as the defence lawyer and when I approached this young man I could see the anxiety in his face because he was warned about how defence council tries to discredit one's evidence. My question to him was "You introduced yourself to this Court as –Special Contable Larat, isn't that right?" "Yes", he replied. I asked "Did your mother give you that name or are you just trying to impress the Judge by introducing yourself as someone special?" He waited for a moment, after all, we taught him to listen to the question, think about his answer and then give his answer. He turned to the judge and said "Your honour, I don't make the rules, I just play the game."

» » **Nothing but the truth** » »

During mock court training a young recruit entered the courtroom with an exhibit in his hands that he intended to enter into evidence. He was asked just before the trial got under way if he wanted to say anything to the judge as he got into the witness stand. The member quickly remarked "Your honour, I want you to know that I lost the exhibit four times."

» » **Memorable quotes on the witness stand** » »

Recruits in training tried their best to present their evidence in mock court exercises. The following are a few quotes that required further explanation:

- "I held him while my partner cuffed him".
- "We were driving down Shaw Street responding to the complaint, and I ran into the complainant. Then we spotted the accused."
- "I began to commence to proceed etc".
- Female member giving evidence on a charge of an offensive weapon. "Your Honour, after arresting the accused, I did a quick search and found a bulge in the front of his pants."
- East Coast Fisheries member - "I was laying down by the creek and they spied me out."

» » **Having your day in court** » »

I charged a guy years ago with driving without due care and attention as I had observed him driving on the wrong side of the road. I discovered he was an Englishman who had recently moved to Canada. This man went to court to fight the charge. I knew I had a good case because I had about 10 separate witnesses who were nearly run down by this man as he came over the crest of a hill. Turns out during the court case, all my witnesses gave their accounts and at the end of this trial the accused got up and gave his evidence. He stated he was sorry and admitted he had driven on the wrong side of the road. The judge promptly asked the accused "Why then, did you plead 'Not Guilty' to the charge?" The accused replied. "I heard in Canada you can always have your day in court". The judge found the accused guilty and issued the appropriate penalty.

»» Severe head trauma ««

A pathologist testifies in court in Mission, B.C. in the 1970's. The case involved an incident where four young men attend a drinking party and sometime during the night one of them falls out of favour with the other three. They proceeded to take turns kicking him in the head and back for a period of about three hours stopping only after they were too tired or intoxicated. The victims skull was completely shattered and his head an unrecognizable pulp. During the murder trial the pathologist gave his evidence describing the injuries sustained and the cause of death. On cross-examination, the following questions were asked by both the defence and the prosecution:

Defence:	"Mr. Pathologist, could these injuries have been caused by a fall?"
Pathologist:	"Yes".
Crown Counsel:	"Mr. Pathologist, what type of fall would it have taken to sustain these types of injuries?"
Pathologist:	"From either a very tall building or from an airplane."
Defence:	"No further questions."

»» Small town court – Time to Pay ««

In the small towns of Alberta, provincial court proceedings were held usually once a month in a local hall. Locals would show up to get a glimpse of who was summoned to appear for certain offences. A travelling Provincial Court Magistrate would preside over the cases and the Detachment Commander or a senior constable would present their cases acting as the prosecution. On more serious cases, Crown Counsel would be brought in to run proceedings on behalf of the Crown. I recall simple charges like illegal possession of liquor were routine from some of the subjects that were summoned to attend court. The usual fine for illegal possession of liquor was $25.00. In one instance, all of the friends of the accused showed up in court for moral support. The judge listened to the circumstances and gave the accused a $50.00 fine and added, in default of payment, 4 days in jail. Sometimes extra court costs were included in the sentence handed out. This caught the accused off guard thinking he would only get a $25.00 fine. The accused asked the judge for time to pay. The judge replied "Does the liquor store ask for time to pay? The accused said "No." The judge than replied "Neither does the court". The accused had to scramble for assistance from his buddies sitting in the gallery to collect the money for the fine.

» » **Walking disjointed** » »

I was instructed to attend my first court case in Winnipeg where I was asked to go and listen to a seasoned member of the Winnipeg Police Service to give evidence. This was part of an In-Service Training exercise. The member of the police service I was fortunate to listen to was known for giving colourful testimony. The case was one of impaired driving. The police constable gave his evidence and made the comment that the suspect was walking in a 'disjointed manner!'

Defence counsel jumped at the chance to get clarification from this witness on what he meant by the description "walking in a disjointed manner". The witness replied "Any time this person moved his feet, it came as a complete surprise to the rest of his body". The accused was convicted.

» » **Proof of age** » »

Only in Alberta would a fellow try and defend himself on a liquor charge. The age of majority in those days for entering a licensed establishment was 21 years. I can recall challenging a young man on his identity after discovering him inside a bar. I pointed out to him that his identification proves that he is only 20 years of age. His reply "Yes I am - but I was sick one year".

» » "I got a record!" » »

I was attending court in a small community in Alberta in the early 1970's. A number of people were gathering and amongst them were different males that happened to be wearing pieces of clothing or pins, hats or paraphernalia that suggested they were members of the RCMP or associated in some way to the RCMP. One person remarked "Are you a member?" to which the reply came, "yes, I am. The gentleman turned to another male who was wearing an RCMP fur cap. "Are you a member?" "No", was the reply. He than turned to a third male sitting nearby and made the statement that everyone seems to be wearing something from the RCMP. He asked the third man, "What have you got from the RCMP?" The man replied "I only got a record".

» » He Looked Guilty » »

A member stationed in Alberta is giving his testimony on the stand. The Defence lawyer asked the question "What did my client look like when you first saw him?" The answer was

"He looked guilty your Honour!"

» » Where is the Bible? » »

I was posted in Fort St. John, B.C. A recruit was told by his trainer several times to go watch court proceedings so that he knew what to expect the first time he would give evidence. It became quite obvious that the recruit had not done this. The recruit was called into the court the first time he had to give evidence. He entered the courtroom and walked straight into the accused box. Prepared to be sworn in, he said to the

Court clerk, "Where is the Bible?" The Court clerk, the Judge, Crown and Defense all burst into laughter.

»» Feeling uncomfortable »»

While posted to the Vernon Detachment General Investigation Section years ago, I investigated a case of an elderly female who was raped after the suspect broke into her residence. I was presenting evidence to a Supreme Court Judge and Jury. Under heated and intense cross examination I was asked to describe the appearance of the accused at the time he was being interrogated by myself after his arrest.

Without hesitation I was able to provide evidence to the courts by stating I felt extremely unsettled, with a dry mouth, and using a nervous but confident tone in my voice. I had a keen desire to remove myself from that very situation. In fact, I requested and was granted a much needed glass of fresh water. I continued to tell the Court that the accused had appeared and felt much like myself at that moment. The Court immediately erupted in laughter and there is no doubt that I had relayed an answer which the Court could appreciate. In the end, a conviction resulted, and to this day, even I must chuckle at just how uncomfortable the accused and myself appeared.

CHAPTER #8

Staffing Interviews

»» **Wrong File** »»

Most all members over the years dreaded staffing interviews. It was widely known that Force policy dictated that every 3 years or so someone from Staffing and Personal Branch would review your personal file and come out to interview you. This was a time for members to discuss their career aspirations and to assess what direction their career should take. In years gone by, Staffing Officers and members from that branch tended to have a lot of input in controlling what kind of comments went into one's personal file. Now that process has check systems so that personal files don't become red tagged with adverse information without justification.

There have been war stories that would make your head spin. I have heard of staffing interviews where the member would come into the interview, pleasantries would be exchanged and the Officer conducting the interview would ask "How are your wife and kids?" The member would be dumb-founded, as he was single, and quickly learned that the Staffing officer had the wrong file in front of him.

»» **Getting the Shaft** »»

For years, the feeling amongst some members was that dealing with Staffing Branch was like Uranium Mining, You couldn't see what they were up to, you knew they were there and all you got was the 'shaft'. It is a pleasure to see that with the access to information legislation members have at last the opportunity to examine the written comments on their personal files. This was not available to members until the late 1970's. I recall looking at my personal file for the first time after being in the Force for 14 yrs. It was quite funny to read the comments investigators put on my file relating to my background checks before I joined the force. They had concerns about my large ears and wondered if I could handle the hassle I would get once becoming a member.

» »   Dull witted and slow thinking   » »

I recall going through the process for being considered a potential applicant for the Vancouver Police Department. I was privy to the interviewer's comments and was surprised by what was written. Quote: "This individual is dull witted, slow thinking and had a problem answering the simplest of questions!" I had just gone through all the hoops and this was my final department interview. I was not a successful candidate. This bad experience led me to apply to another police department which resulted in my successful entry into policing.

» »   No Interest   » »

I had a dim view of Staffing and Personnel after experiencing my Staffing Officer focus more on looking out the Detachment window which overlooked a soccer field. He appeared more interested in what was going on during the soccer game than giving attention to my career. It is a wonder I survived to go as far as I did in the organization.

Form A-26

The assessment form used by the RCMP was Form A-26. Supervisors and trainers would hang this carrot in front of those they did assessments on to encourage them to meet job expectations. This put a lot of stress on members when it came to their yearly assessment date.

Rating Scale

I once had a sergeant who told everyone on the shift during performance reviews, no one would ever get a "5" rating. He would say that to get a "5" rating you had to be perfect and only God was that good. During my next performance review when we came to the category on attendance, I challenged him about my "4" rating. I asked if I had ever missed a day at work? If he had ever had to remind me about booking annual leave or any other time off that was allowed? Had I ever been late for work? He answered "No" to all of these questions. I then asked what I could do better to get a higher rating. He didn't answer and just gave me a "5" rating. The next year attendance was no longer a category on the performance review.

Never Got Laid

An interview with a new recruit in the field by a supervisor went something like this. The recruit had already experienced a lot of "On Call" duty at a Detachment. When asked how he has enjoyed his first few months of experience at the Detachment, his reply was: "I've never had my pants off so many times in one day and never even got laid!"

Stat Man

I had my yearly assessment interview with my superior officer in North Vancouver in the early 1970's. He was a great "stat" man. He had read my assessment and noted that I was not one to give many traffic tickets. I was very quick to reply. I told him that he was correct but he should also be aware that my tickets were never contested either. He looked at me and just smiled.

» » "That's the year I got shot!" » »

During a yearly staffing interview at the Delta Police Department, the senior officer briefly looked at a member's file and remarked to the member "I see here you took quite a bit of sick leave in 1986" There was a pause… the member thinks for a second and says "Ya.. that's the year I got shot!" The reply he heard from the officer was "Of Course!" Just another example of how well a senior officer might look at a member's personnel file before a yearly interview.

» » You're Transferred! » »

In 1978 I was stationed in Prince George Detachment and only had one year service. I get a call one morning while on shift. It's a representative from North American Van Lines telling me he has me slated to move me to Fort St. James Detachment. This was the first I had heard of this as I had not heard from Staffing about this. That is when the fellow on the phone says, "Oh, – I'm sorry, I was not supposed to phone you until at least 1:00 p.m.". I felt I had been pranked.

Within an hour I get a call from Staffing and Personnel out of Victoria. I was told there was an opening for a position in Fort St. James with a request to have me consider a transfer to that Detachment. It was evident Staffing had already pre-arranged for the mover to give me a call. In those days you never challenged Staffing & Personnel.

CHAPTER #9

Keeping Sane On Midnight Shift

»» It's only an ambulance »»

Coquitlam Detachment dispatch reports a complaint of a speeding ambulance on the Loughheed Hwy going 160 mph. I find the ambulance and ticket him and then go back to the office to advise the dispatcher that there are few if any vehicles capable of going 160 mph. The dispatcher is not convinced as she says she knows someone who has a Corvette that does 160 mph. I decide it is time to convince this dispatcher of the error of her ways. With the aid of 5 other members and with the knowledge and consent of the NCO's, I wait until about 3:00 a.m. and call in that I am stopping a white car at Blue Mountain Road and Lougheed Hwy. Then I announce the white car is running and that I am in pursuit. The 5 other members call in that they are approaching Lougheed Hwy to assist and they call in their positions as being #1, #2, #3, #4, & #5 which are about 1 1/2 miles apart or supposedly 7 ½ to 8 miles along the highway. In fact, they were only stretched over a distance of about 2 miles or 1/4 of what they reported. They would then key their radio mike and announce my passing their position as I would drive by at 60 mph, full siren of course. Thinking that they were further apart the dispatcher thought I was going 4X 60 = 240 mph. She was about to alert the neighboring Detachment when the NCO advised her not to. She figured something was afoot and radioed my car. I could hear her voice had changed so I said "Cancel that pursuit Brenda - it was only an Ambulance!"

»» Cat Bridging »»

In one policing jurisdiction, one member would befriend a strange cat that was on the loose. He would place the cat in the trunk of the police car and drive around for a while to ensure the cat had a definite urge to get out asap. The member would than summon his comrades to meet him at a location along the river bank. He would back the police car up and hit the trunk button releasing the trunk latch. The rest who showed up would watch a cat jump out of the trunk into the middle of thin air in a frantic effort to escape her capture but only to find the landing to be the river. The cat survived.

»» Wink of an eye »»

My partner and I were conducting a long surveillance on a target. The hours went by slowly. We would talk about a lot of things as the time went by. I was married and she was single. She is sitting back in the passenger seat slouched somewhat so as not be too conspicuous.

We see no activity on the part of the target and are wondering how long this surveillance should continue. As time goes by and nothing is said, she finally throws this question in my direction:

"What winks like a pussy cat and screws like a tiger?" I replied I had no idea and all she did was "wink" at me. That was it. It was time to shut the evening down and call an end to this surveillance exercise.

»» Wings anyone! »»

When it was really dead quiet, in the middle of the night, my trainer and I used to go to the larger neighbouring community for wings from a 7-11 store. My trainer would always throw the wings out the window as he was eating them. One day, I got into the vehicle we had driven and noted a chicken wing on the floor so I told my Corporal we needed to get the vehicle cleaned. The Cpl. went out to the truck and scooped the ill-fated wing and placed it, ever so neatly, back in my trainer's basket. My poor trainer!

» » One finger salute » »

Certain members take specialized training to become 'Identification Specialists', They are called to crime scenes to collect evidence and obtain prints, take photos and prepare a detailed outline of a crime scene. One such member has put in a long day in Saskatchewan and is driving home from a call in the middle of the night trying to stay awake. It is 20 degrees below zero or better. He tries to focus on things on the road as light snowflakes are coming at him in the headlights. He felt like he was traveling in space. His eye catches the image of what seems to be a leather glove laying on the paved roadway in front of him. He slows down to try and focus and allow his left front tire to drive over the glove just to see if his driving skills are still sharp; After-all he was pretty good at hitting gophers in the Summer this way. He drives over the glove and quickly checks his rear view mirror to confirm he had actually hit his target. What he saw woke him up, as the glove had moved upon driving over it which for some reason caused the middle finger portion of the glove to come straight up as if it give him the 'one finger salute'. This image stuck in his mind for a long time as he continued on his patrol back home that night.

» » The Plan » »

This document has floated about Detachment offices for years when members were poking fun at management for some of the policy decisions made within the organization.

"THE PLAN"

In the beginning was 'The Plan', and then came the Assumptions, and the Assumptions were without form, and the Plan was completely without substance, and the darkness was upon the faces of the Constables, and they spoke unto their Sergeants, saying: "It is a crock of shit and it stinketh."

And the Sergeants went unto their respective Staff Sergeants saying: "It is a pail of excrement and none may abide by the odor thereof."

And the Staff Sergeants went unto their Inspectors and did sayeth unto them: "It is a container of dung and it is very strong such that none may abide by it."

And the Inspectors went unto their Staff/Inspectors and did sayeth unto them: "It is a vessel of fertilizer and none may abide by its strength."

And the Staff/Inspectors went unto their Superintendents and did speak thus: "It contains much which aids plant growth and it is very strong in a certain aspect."

And the Deputy Chiefs went unto the Chief and spoke thusly unto him: "This powerful new plan will actively promote growth and efficiency in all respects and in this area in particular."

And the Chief looked upon the Plan and saw that is was good and 'The Plan' became policy.

» » Revised Police Warning » »

After the Charter of Rights came into play in 1982, members jokingly made up formats for how official police warnings should look like. This one joking version surfaced and was cause for conversation and chuckle around the briefing rooms.

Police Services Division is now recommending that police officers use the following wording for the "Right to Counsel" caution:

I am arresting you for _____ (read the reasons for the arrest directly from the criminal code in French and English.) It is my duty to inform you that you have the right to retain and instruct counsel without delay. You have the right to telephone a lawyer you wish. It is my duty to ask if you are feeling depressed about your current arrest. 1-800-265-0452 is a toll-free number that will put you in contact with a legal aid psychologist, free of charge. You also have the right to free advice from a legal aid lawyer. 1-800-265-0451 is a toll-free number that will put in contact with a legal aid duty counsel lawyer for free legal advice. It is also my duty to ask if all is well with your family and pets at home. 1-800-265-0453 is a toll-free number that will put you in contact with a veterinarian for free advice in relation to the health of your pets. Also, how is your car running? I have a list of reasonably-priced mechanics who will inspect your vehicle at this time. Are you hungry at this time? If so, I will buy you something to eat because your welfare is my highest priority. Do you understand? Do you wish to call a lawyer, psychologist, veterinarian or mechanic now? Do you wish to drive the cruiser to the Detachment?

CHAPTER #10

Practical Jokes Played

»» **GOTCHA!!!** »»

This one Corporal I worked with was my supervisor. He was noted to be a very meticulous man getting fussy about the little things going on during the shift. It was time to get even. Members observed the Corporal show up at the Sub office and leave his briefcase in the P.C. (Police Cruiser).

They waited long enough to ensure he was busy in the office and than set the plan into action. They even got the Identification specialist involved on this one. They left the sub office and took everything out of the Cpl's. P.C. including his briefcase, shotgun etc. They rolled the driver window down and made it look like someone had smashed the window to gain entry into the police transport. The Identification member assisted by supplying some broken auto safety glass to spread inside the P.C.

The poor Cpl. was observed as having a near breakdown because of what he had discovered when he left the Sub office. He arranged to have the identification member attend to, take pictures and examine the scene. As the Cpl. was watching one member remarked "I wonder what kind of prints we could get off the driver's side window? At this point, the Identification member commences to roll up the driver's side front window and the rest of the members watching told the Cpl. "GOTCHA!!!".

» » Set up flares » »

It was always neat to try and suck a new rookie into doing something foolish at their new posting. Here is an example of one prank we exposed them to. Similar pranks have been played out at other detachments over the years, each with their own level of humorous outcome. We would wait until the appropriate time the rookie was beginning to feel comfortable while on shift. We picked an evening where there was a foggy night with low cloud cover and weather conditions were poor. Dispatch radio was also in on the prank and the stage was set. Radio communications were directed to this member to prepare an area where it was safe to land a helicopter. He was instructed to go to a certain shopping centre and light up the area appropriately with road flares so the helicopter pilot could plainly see where to land. After the rookie set up the flares, he would contact Dispatch and report that he could not hear or see any signs of a helicopter approaching. After some time had elapsed the rest of the patrol units would show up at the scene and congratulate the rookie for giving it his best shot. There was an immediate vow by the rookie to get even.

» » Getting sucked in » »

A similar set of circumstances surrounded giving a young member instructions to stand outside the Detachment with a flashlight and to wait for the aircraft to come flying over the Detachment as the pilot did not know if the landing gear was functioning or not. A visual inspection was requested. A few members have been sucked in on this one over the years.

» » Screwing around » »

One of my favorite tricks was done on several occasions during my career. We would arrange to have someone from the plain clothes section come into the police office and approach the front counter where we made sure that the rookie was working.

The member playing the part of the complainant would look upset and blurt out "I want to see the member that has been screwing around with my wife.". The rookie in one instance replied "Did you wish to speak to the Sgt. sir?"

At this the complainant replied "Is that the son of a bitch?" and at the same time made gestures that he was going to come over the counter. We would then come to the aid of the rookie and again congratulate them on a job well done.

» »   **Getting Even**   » »

Members I used to work with at one posting were always uptight because all the drunks were downtown and the members working the residential areas never got any calls to match what we had to put up with. It was time to teach them that they needed their share as well. One night after receiving a call of a drunk at a certain location downtown, a patrol was made by a colleague of mine only to find this poor individual completely out of it and pitifully dirty as he had relieved himself from both ends. This subject was loaded into the police transport and taken to the residential side of town where he was removed and placed in a comfortable position at a given location near a hotel where we knew the drunk would be safe. An anonymous call was placed by this member indicating that a drunk was noted at a certain location. He then sat back and watched the boys make their patrol and find the subject. One small step towards getting even with the boys on the other side of town. Subject was taken to cells for the night.

» »   **Halloween dummy**   » »

On the night shift before Halloween I had arrested two guys for breaking into a Dry Cleaners in Maple Ridge. One guy resisted and was subdued with my 3 cell flashlight. The NCO, upon hearing about my arrest questioned whether that might have been excessive force but as there were two of them and no back up it never went any further.

The next night shift is Halloween. A very large Auxiliary member and I are on patrol and are dispatched to a 'Body on Road' complaint. We attend to find some genius had put a "Dummy", fully clothed, wig, shoes etc., on the road to perhaps cause someone to go off the road. We take the dummy back to the office where I request assistance with a (J3), which is the radio code for prisoner in custody. The same NCO that questioned me about excessive use of force the night before came to assist. I took the opportunity to set the NCO up by staging what might appear to be an assault on my prisoner, (the dummy). As the NCO opens the door to the cell block area he sees the Auxiliary member hold the "prisoner" / dummy in a full nelson position and I am going through the motions of just *nailing* this dummy. The Sgt. runs out and grabs me to stop me only to find out it was a dummy.

He decided he would not be the last victim of the prank so we hung the dummy in the female cell which had a solid door. You could just see the hair, of the wig and the rope above the door.

For the next 8 hours (every few minutes), we had members come in and try and identify the J3 we had in this cell. The reactions varied from freezing, fainting, to the Cpl. who came in, walked back out, hung up the keys, went to the exit and yelled "Your prisoner has hung himself and I wasn't here!"

» » Sex Change dilemma » »

When I was working the front counter at our detachment one of my responsibilities was to process criminal records checks. I was a single female so all the guys used to play jokes on me all the time. I answered the phone and the conversation went like this:

Me»   RCMP front desk, Bonjour.
Him»   "Is this line recorded?"
Me»   "No"
Him»   "Do you have call display?"

Me»	"No, why are you asking Sir?"
Him»	"I need to speak to whoever does the criminal record checks."
Me»	"I do them, how can I help you?"
Him»	"Do you give out any of that information to anyone?"
Me»	"Only to the person who requested the information."
Him»	"Can you tell on your computer systems if someone has changed their name legally?"
Me»	"Well it depends. We would treat that as an alias name, if we knew that you had one."
Him»	"I'll tell you what happened. I had a sex change operation years ago and have recently had to request a criminal records check on myself for work reasons. Someone here at work made a comment to me that made me think he knows that I had this sex change. Do you guys have that information about who has sex change operations??"
Me»	(and you can imagine how I'm reacting to this), "Well sir, I think I would definitely remember seeing that bit of information cross my desk."
Him»	"Well the only two people who know I've had this done are myself and the Dr. who performed the operation. I'm married and my wife doesn't even know."
Me»	"Wow."
Him»	"Yeah, so you can see why I'm so concerned that this information is not accessible by anyone."
Me»	(mind racing), "No, there is nothing here that I've seen that would indicate that we've checked you under your male and female name."
Him»	"Yeah.... well this guy is really on to me here at work. I know he knows. I'm even scared to take a piss beside him in the bathroom now. I think he's trying to eye me up to see if I have breasts."
Me»	(now I'm thinking this is one of the jerks upstairs yanking my chain)
Me»	"That would be a problem.

Him»   "So I can assume this secret is safe with you?"
Me»   "Oh my, yes"

And that was it. To this day, the guys at the office all deny making the call to me....

That's why if you're going to crack up laughing, always put the caller on hold first!

» »   Stolen Blue Ford   » »

Selkirk Municipal Detachment had about 20 members at the time. In those days, the night guards were also dispatchers and complaint takers. Mike was the man, highly educated and recently retired from a career with steel manufacturing company. He decided to become a part-time night guard. He answered calls and dispatched them to the two cars on the road. He did CPIC and Motor Vehicle Branch checks for us.

With the extra income from the night guard job, Mike purchased a brand new Ford Custom vehicle. The Ford was clearly Mike's pride and joy. He cleaned and polished it every day. One night, out of boredom, the other town police member and I met behind the Detachment and noted Mike's car at the end of the parking lot. He parked the Ford away from the police cars so he wouldn't get any dents in it. The other member decided to play a joke on the old night guard, and I played along. We had our own "local" frequency and nobody monitored us other than the night guard.

We called in a blue Ford, possibly stolen, being driven erratically and gave Mike's licence plate number. Seconds later we said that we were in pursuit and were headed north out of town at high speed. Mike didn't say anything but we knew he was listening. Eventually we said that the car had rolled over on Whiskey ditch road and that we would be out of the car.

It took a few minutes but eventually Mike came outside and saw his car parked at the end of the parking lot. He kind of "trotted" to his car, walked around and even bent over to check his licence plate. Then he noticed us parked behind the detachment; we were both laughing. Mike was mad for a moment, and then laughed. He realized how silly he had been with his new car. The following night, the Ford was parked beside everybody else's car in the parking lot.

» » "We're going to die" » »

If you ever want to wake up your partner, this one worked for me. We were working a midnight shift and my partner was nodding off to the point of falling asleep. I waited until he was pretty well into his cycle of sleep when I pulled up into a truck stop and just in front of a semitrailer truck that was just parked with its headlights on. As I approached the parked semitrailer truck and braced myself for an interesting reaction from my partner. I slightly hit the breaks and hung unto the steering wheel yelling out "We're going to die!". The millisecond of thought that must have gone through my partner's head when he opened up his eyes may have burned an image that he will probably never forget. We both had a good laugh over this incident.

» » Ask no questions » »

Back in 1982 while at Coquitlam Detachment, I was on my own for probably the first or second time. I was feeling sexy and fully competent as a Police Officer even though I really knew nothing. Two well respected General Investigation Section (GIS) guys requested my assistance. I immediately indicated I was in the area and could help. Upon getting to Lafarge Lake the two GIS guys emerged from the woods, sweaty and with ties askew asked for my revolver. I was to ask no questions and simply give them my gun. Being new and afraid to question two seasoned police officers, no less in plain clothes, I gave them my gun. They retreated to the woods where I heard 2 shots. They emerged from the wooded area and told me to go back to shift, clear my gun and never speak another word of what just occurred.

What really occurred was that the two GIS guys were required to put two slugs into a bear cadaver for later exhumation and study. This was done so that they may gain expertise in this regard. They thought why not have some fun with this and suck in a young recruit along the way.

In the meantime I was not having a comfortable shift. I held my own until I got home where I sat down to have dinner with my wife who happened to be a police officer in an adjoining jurisdiction.

The two Police Officers who set me up took it a step further and had a contact at my wife's work location casually asking her if she had heard anything about two members involved in a shooting where I worked in Coquitlam. She simply mentioned it during casual conversation that night. After feeling lightheaded and barely able to finish my dinner I went to bed as I had to get up early for a shift the next day. I probably slept a total of 2 hours that night and hesitantly went to work in the morning.

I was met at the back door of the office by another GIS member who requested he needed to speak to me on an urgent manner. He also asked for my gun (which by the way I had not cleaned!!) Upon 5 minutes of silence in the interview room and the Cpl. examining my gun, the door burst open with 3-5 fellow members laughing. I knew the gig was up and after a few minutes to compose myself, laughed as well.

» » **Door prize** » »

In the early 1970's a young constable nicknamed "Rogy", organized, hosted and was the MC for a Kamloops City Detachment social function. This dance gave members and close friends of the Force a chance to get together and blow off a little steam. Rogy had coordinated prizes to be given out to lucky winners throughout the evening. There was a door prize, the eligibility for which was simply an entry ticket and attendance. In order to win one of the other two prizes you had to purchase prize tickets being sold throughout the course of the evening, one being a washer and dryer and the other a color T.V. Terrific prizes for this social evening. Ticket sales went extremely well, considering. One lady, who had always been very vocal, spent a fortune on tickets and was the recipient of the first prize drawn.. The washer and dryer. She nearly went nuts when Rogy presented her with a very large metal round washer complete with hole and a dish towel wrapped in it. She was not pleased. You might guess, the remaining prizes were a colour spray painted very old broken portable T.V. and an actual "Door" as a door prize. The funds collected for the prizes went to offset costs for the social evening and a few other prizes handed out that evening. All in all, a very good cause. One additional fact: Rogy was the local fraud investigator at the Detachment.

» » Kit & Clothing order » »

When my co-worker, another recruit, first arrived at the small Northern community in the Prairies that I policed, his trainer decided to play a good joke on him. The recruit's box of kit and clothing had arrived at the office before the recruit arrived. The trainer painstakingly took off the tape from the kit box so it didn't look altered. Then he removed all the RCMP clothes and replaced them with clothes from the lost and found. What was really great was that the recruit's mother was helping the new recruit set up and she got to unload the box, all neatly taped up again. She put the clothes in the closet like she was supposed to. Imagine the recruit's surprise to find old shirts and pants stinking up his closet.

» » Dead Opossum » »

I had placed what I had thought was a dead opossum in a local firemen's truck when they stopped for coffee. As they entered the vehicle after the coffee break the animal had awakened to scare the hell out of them. They had no idea how this occurred but knew some prank had been pulled on them.

» » I'm a Dork! » »

One of the members in our Sub Office placed a sign in the back window of a member's police car that read "I'm a Dork!!" - It took a while before the member actually noticed this as he had a bad habit of not checking his rear view mirror. I am sure the passing motorists got a good chuckle out of viewing the sign inside the back window of a police car.

»» Fart in a Bag! »»

In Yorkton, Saskatchewan, a gentleman came to the front counter of the Detachment claiming someone was trying to kill him. Members knew this person as a regular who had some mental health issues, so they would go out of their way to give him the impression that they would look into his concerns. As the member at the front counter spoke to this complainant, it became obvious to him that the complainant was out to lunch with his allegation. "What makes you think someone is trying to kill you?", he asked. The complainant indicated perhaps it was something he ate because lately whenever he passed gas, the smell was very unusual. The member took advantage of this opportunity and quickly took a calling card from another member's desk and gave it to the complainant along with a garbage bag and a twist tie.

The member's instructions to the complainant was to ensure that whenever he had the urge to pass gas again at home, he should quickly capture the gas he passes into the garbage bag, tie it tightly and immediately deliver the bag as an exhibit to the Yorkton Hospital laboratory office. He was instructed to have the hospital staff at the laboratory call the member whose name appeared on the calling card to get further instructions on what to do with the results of the tests. The complainant was satisfied with these instructions and left. On the next dayshift, the member whose name was on the calling card gets a call from the hospital lab staff enquiring. "We have a man at the lab with a fart in a bag and he wants it analyzed with results passed on to you. What is going on here?" The member discovered who the subject was, and quickly realized one of his partners had played a trick on him."

Office Shenanigans

I was behind one evening, and I desperately wanted to get my paperwork done and to go home. I was tired. Recognizing this, another member, a real prankster, started intentionally asking stupid questions of me, knowing that his efforts were driving me mad, but he persisted. Enough was enough!.... I reached for the first thing on my desk, but my training taught me that throwing scissors might cause injury. Meanwhile the prankster hid behind a filing cabinet across the room. The second item I picked up was a bottle of "Whiteout"... I hurled the bottle at my target.

The neck of the bottle hit the edge of the file cabinet, shattering the lid and spewing the contents all over the member, the wall, the filing cabinet and the rug. Have you ever tried to clean Whiteout out of carpet!? Needless to say I had some explaining to do to my Sergeant the next day.

Out of Order

In our Department it was common to see a few officers in the office take off during the lunch hour for a lunch hour run. They would prance off in their running gear probably trying to impress those under their command that fitness was an important factor in a healthy working environment.

One of the guys on the Watch took note of this ritual and figured he would set up a surprise for them one day. He made up some signs that read "Out of Order - Electrical Fault", and stuck them on the side walls of the shower stalls in the men's change room. When the officers came back from their run all sweaty and ready for their showers, they discovered their dilemma. They were certainly disappointed with the inconvenience. It soon became obvious amongst the rank and file that these fellows did not fall for the practical joke and were not impressed. Others on shift came away that day with a good laugh.

» » Tight Squeeze » »

A member on our Watch used to come off the road when it was his turn to work relief in the Communications Centre. He would quickly take his duty belt off and lay it aside for the shift. One of his fellow officers would find the right time to sneak into his working area, grab the duty belt and synch it up a notch or two. When this guy was finished with his shift he would quickly put on his duty belt only to discover he felt like he had put on a few pounds, and struggled to readjust his belt.

» » Sending a Message » »

One of the members we worked with in the Edmonton Police Service was a bit of a problem member for the squad. He had a very high opinion of himself which got a few of us up tight. Some of the guys on the squad thought they would try and send him a message. They found a dead cat and tied it to the rear of his private vehicle. He apparently drove home from work that day and was stopped by some passer by people who accused him of being some kind of sick individual. He showed up for work the next day pretty upset at everyone for pulling this trick on him. "What goes around – comes around!".

» » Check your weapon » »

One Sunday evening at a posting in northern Alberta my partner and I were doing paper work in the office. My partner had to go to the bathroom so he got up, removed his gun belt and put it on the desk. Off he went. I took his gun out of the holster and handcuffs and hung his gun up near the ceiling using his handcuffs. The weapon hung over the desk of a not so enthusiastic member. (of course the shells were removed). My partner returned and put his belt back on, not noticing his hardware had been removed, then went back to do his typing. A short while later a couple of other members arrived at the office. They immediately noticed the gun hanging. I mentioned to them not to say anything.

My partner said something and we all started laughing and could not stop. The joke was on him and he didn't realize it. The joking continued. My partner at last noticed the hanging gun. He asked whose it was. I told him it was some other member's gun who was on duty and it had been hanging since 5:00 p.m. (it was now 11:30 p.m.).

My partner continually said "How stupid could a member be not to notice that his gun was missing. This went on for about 15 minutes. We convinced my partner to go out of coffee at the local truck stop. As we were sitting at the coffee shop, my partner again said to me – "How could anyone be so fricken stupid, at the same time reaching to touch his gun to indicate one should always be able to feel it. As he did this he found it was actually his gun that was hanging in the office. The red face expression at that moment was priceless.

» » Myra Mains » »

I worked with a member from New Westminster Police Service who was quite religious and for the most part a pretty serious fellow. Someone on the shift had left a message for him to call the local Funeral Home and make enquiries about a recently deceased subject by the name of Myra Mains. After the call, the member soon learned he was set up for the call and was not a happy camper for being made a fool of.

» » First Autopsy » »

Many recruits during their first tour of duty are given an opportunity to attend an autopsy or are given a tour of the local morgue as they will no doubt encounter future cases where they will meet the necessary contacts for follow-up on an investigation. In this instance a member had made arrangements to ensure an autopsy was already in progress but brought with him a can of pork and beans which he somehow placed in the chest cavity of the deceased in the morgue. When the recruit was brought in to show him what the place was all about, one of the members that went with him dipped his fingers into the chest cavity and helped himself to eating a small handful of beans. To say the least the recruit witnessing this action could not believe his eyes and nearly got sick on site. A good laugh was had by all.

CHAPTER #11

Applicants - Interviews

»» **Worst / Best Experience** »»

Members throughout their career get the opportunity to interview individuals who have an interest in joining the Mounted Police. Some have an idea of what police work is all about, and others have not got a clue. Some applicants wish only to become volunteers or apply to be part of support staff. Here are some flashbacks on interviews I've conducted.

It was always a challenge to instil in the mind of the applicant that we were not naive to the pressure young people had in growing up, especially in the last 20 years. I would come around to asking my applicants how many times they have used soft drugs and quickly threw in the figure 10 to 20 times. You could see them analyzing the question and most would respond with what probably was a truthful answer in admitting some use.

I recall asking during interviews what their worst or best experience was in their life. Sometimes I would ask them about what their most stressful moment was in their life. Here are some answers:

WORST: "When my dad took my dog away". *** "When my mother died". *** "My divorce" *** "Getting shot at in Cypress" *** "Having a bad car accident". **** "Working in a negative job environment" *** "Getting fired." *** "This interview!"
BEST: "Getting my Degree". *** "Getting married". *** "It hasn't happened yet". *** "Getting my drivers license".

» »   I Promise   » »

One of my colleagues had the opportunity to interview a visible minority who wanted to become a member. During his conversation with this man an issue came up that caused my colleague to challenge the applicant as to how truthful he really was in giving information about his background. The applicant knew he was cornered and replied "I know I haven't been honest with you, but I promise to be once I become a policeman!".

» »   I don't like the Prairies   » »

During one interview with a young man who expressed an interest in making an application for the RCMP, I asked him "What would make you quit the Force" He leaned forward, tapped my desk with his two right hand fingers and replied "Two things…. I don't like the Prairies and I can't stand flying!" I thought to myself – you poor sucker. I didn't have the heart to tell him he would spend 6 months in Regina, Saskatchewan and we would probably fly him there. He never pursued his application into the Force.

» »   Exhausted   » »

Brandon Police Service - During our selection process in Brandon, several of the steps are done, one after the other, to accommodate out-of-town candidates. During this one particular selection process we were running the physical testing and then doing an interview soon after.

This one candidate had completed the physical testing. He went off and showered and changed, then went directly into the interview process. He was answering all the questions well when suddenly after a question he just sat there with this blank stare.

The interviewer asked the question again and he just sat there. The interviewer went over to check him and he just fell over out of his chair.

An ambulance was called and the candidate was fine. Apparently he had not eaten at all that morning and after the physical testing his body was exhausted. He went to have something to eat and came back in the afternoon to complete his interview.

» »   Still wants the job   » »

At my small rural first posting, I was in charge of doing background checks on all potential guards and matrons. One day, a local person came in who was new to the North moving in from Regina. He asked to become a guard so I gave him the necessary paperwork, told him to fill it out and come back. Later, I reviewed some of it with him and noted he had a pretty lengthy criminal record. I told him I would have to do some additional background checks and I would get back to him. Police records reflected a long list of criminal offences including armed standoff with police. He was called back and informed we had no guard job to offer him at this time.

» »   A Go-getter   » »

When I first started working in Staffing & Personnel branch, I reviewed the files of regular members and also conducted recruiting interviews. I recall interviewing an applicant for a position of a Civilian Member within the Force. This one was unique as he was in a wheelchair. All his credentials looked good and met what the Force was looking for. One of my co-workers came up to me after the interview and asked what I thought of the individual to which I replied in French "Y roule en tabarnak!" The term in French meant he was a go-getter and motivated, but its other meaning also could mean that he could be rolling along quite nicely.

» »   Surprise home visit   » »

Brandon Police Service - Hiring Process. During the background investigation, one of the steps in the selection process requires investigators to do a surprise home visit to see how the candidate lives. In this one case, while checking out the candidate's apartment the investigator noticed drug paraphernalia in one of the bedrooms. When asked about it the candidate stated that it was his roommate's bedroom and that the roommate did not smoke marijuana in front of him. If the roommate was going to smoke up he would go out to his car and do it. Needless to say, we didn't hire this one.

» » Circumcision - Not a requirement » »

You get all kinds of individuals applying for the RCMP. I recall one who wrote in and enquired whether a person has to be circumcised in order to be an applicant over and above all the other requirements of height and eyesight.

» » Polygraph test failed » »

A regular member applicant shows up for his scheduled polygraph test in Vancouver. The polygraph operator asks him "When was the last time you used any drugs?". The applicant's reply was "This morning – I took a little cocaine to clear my head!" His application process was discontinued.

» » Blackmail » »

During a recent security interview conducted with an applicant I asked the question "Have you ever done anything in your past that would subject you to blackmail or coercion? The applicant hesitated for a second and replied "I have never had an affair with a black male before". The applicant had to be given a clearer explanation of what 'blackmail' and 'coercion' meant by definition.

CHAPTER #12

Gone Are The Days When

» »   **Up in smoke**   » »

It's mid-winter and the start of the day shift. Everyone is heading out in the morning to start the police transports so they could warm up. Fifteen minutes passed and one of the members looks outside to check the vehicles. Two looked like they were in good shape with the frost gone on the windows. He remarked that one of the police cars wasn't warming up yet because the frost was not off the windows. Upon closer examination it was noted that one police car referred to was full of smoke. The portable spotlight was left on the front seat and because of the intense heat produced by the spotlight, it had burned a hole in the front seat.

There have been many members including myself who were held responsible for repair of seat covers when we accidentally left the spotlight on, causing a near fire in the police car. Members however found ways to pay for the repair costs. We would buy a bottle of Crown Royal whiskey and sell raffle tickets to the guys on the Watch during the shift. Proceeds went towards the cost of repair because the Force wouldn't pay for it. There were times we would be buying raffle tickets regularly to cover each other's costs. After a while some front seats in police cars looked like patchwork quilting. A local leather upholsterer would accommodate us in taking on a minor repair job.

» » Watch your language » »

The Cpl. in charge of the Watch in Kamloops, B.C. made an interesting discovery. He noticed that the guys I worked with were swearing a little too much while on shift. It was his intent to have us change our behaviour by advising us to come up with some new words to replace those common swear words we were using. We responded by coming up with the following:

"Rotten GASNARF" -was a term used to describe anyone who had no class and was deemed worthless; An individual who might pick his nose and eat it.

"GAZORNAPLAT" - was a term we used to describe the lowest thing on earth. Members used their imagination to add their own meanings. I found that as we took advantage of the new vocabulary, we had people wondering what we were really saying, and at the same time we kept the vulgar language out of our routine conversation. Thirty years later when some of the same fellows meet each other they still make the odd reference to calling each other a "Rotten Gasnarf" or a "Gazornaplat".

ADMINISTRATION MANUAL: 1.4.D.4.d.

Officers,... will return a salute
when you are saluted (EXEPTION:
Do not return a salute when your
sword is drawn.) ...

»» Avoiding the salute »»

During the Mid 1970's a certain high ranking officer in Kamloops Sub-Division had this hang-up about being saluted any time he was approached by a regular member. Members took every opportunity not to wear their hats after getting out of their police car when they knew there was an officer nearby. For some reason there was this fear that one would have to salute the officer, so you would usually see the guys carry their hats in their arms as they were coming into the office. I was one of these guys and got caught in the hallway coming into the office. The officers remarks were similar to "What's the matter Constable, scared to wear your hat today?"

»» Putting on the Miles »»

There were times that great pains were taken to get rid of older police transports that ran like junkers. Head Quarters policy however, would indicate you had to have a certain amount of mileage registered before you could submit reports requesting a replacement vehicle. Several members have indicated that in earlier years in order to get rid of a Junker that still had a few miles left before being eligible for replacement, they would make arrangements to jack the rear of the police transport up so that the car could run in high gear at idle for a while.

If you left the vehicle running for a long period of time you had quite a few miles chalked up over the weekend. What an opportunity to let H.Q. know what kind of weekend patrols you made and at the same time you came closer to that magical target so you could get a new police car.

»» Last Chance »»

A member stationed in a small northern BC community got so fed up with dealing with the same guy day in and day out that he decided to take the fellow out of town and into the bush. There he had a chat with the fellow, and told him he was at his wit's end in wondering what to do with the man. He told the fellow that he had no choice but to consider doing him in. He thought for a moment and than told this individual that he was a man of fair play and would give the fellow a chance to survive.

He advised the man that he would allow him to start running into the bush while he counted to three. He let the man start running, counted one…. Two… three… and than fired his revolver into the sky three times. The man disappeared into the bush and was not seen in the community for some time. This member used what he thought was the best approach to keeping a lid on things in his community.

» » Less than compassionate » »

Gone are the days when I felt sympathy for persons repeatedly in custody. The biggest turning point for me happened a few months ago when I was getting a ride home from work. I escort prisoners for a living. I was so shocked during the event that I did not even react until it was too late. I was the passenger in the vehicle.

We were stopped at a red light, and were closest to the centre line on a four lane road in the downtown core of Vancouver. We were discussing our day when I noticed a lady on the sidewalk. I recognized her, as she was frequently arrested for misdemeanors. I was just saying how I felt sympathy for her, as I thought she was one of the few that could really use the extra assistance. Then she looked in my direction and I could actually see the look in her eyes change to sheer anger. She recognized me as a sheriff and in lightning speed ran through traffic at our vehicle. In an instant she was banging on our vehicle. I was absolutely amazed at her behavior, she then yelled at me through the open window and then spat in my face. Traffic had begun moving and our vehicle was now blocking it, so, without getting out of the car to deal with her, I told my friend to drive away. I think I said that partly out of shock, and partly due to it being Friday, I just wanted to go home. This event gave me a whole new view towards people involved in criminal activity. Being a person employed within the judicial system,

I have had compassion for the perpetrators. However, now as a victim of an offence, I feel less than compassionate.

»» I have the honour – Sir! »»

I recall writing at the bottom of a memo headed for Head Quarters with my usual request for approval on something. One of the last things we had to write on the bottom of the memo was "I have the honour, Sir, of being your obedient servant!" This statement was expected to be inserted in a memorandum whenever a member was making an application for special leave or a request to get married. This practice slowly disappeared around the mid to late 1960's and demonstrated at that time how some senior officers demanded respect, even on paper.

»» "Head Smashed In" »»

The following article was submitted by a retired S/Sgt. for the RCMP Quarterly Magazine.

Peer at the cliff where millions of buffalo plunged to their deaths at Alberta's Head Smashed-In Buffalo Jump and it's easier to understand how a massive animal, one who dominated the prairies for centuries, was reduced to today's smattering in a few protected areas.

The buffalo might have survived had it not been for the European influx – white buffalo hunters and pioneers hungry for large tracts of farm land. The Indians killed more than they needed, approaching on foot and herding many buffalo toward the edge – stampeding them at the last moment so their momentum carried them to their deaths – wasn't exactly considered a conservation maneuver, but was very efficient.

As I mused, I thought of another western icon: the Royal Canadian Mounted Police.

This worthy and durable organization has been a fundamental building block of my personal being. My father joined in 1930 and policed all parts of Canada for 35 years. I followed in his footsteps in 1961, serving 33 years from coast to coast. My son recently completed training and is embarking on his own career. It was presumed that his future in the force was assured.

The buffalo analogy is ominous. Once they began running, nothing could stop their great momentum and prevent their rush over the precipice. A similar fate may be in store for the RCMP. Momentum is building and they soon may be 'over the edge;' this is particularly ironic as the plains buffalo is an RCMP symbol.

Canada's increased population and complexity has overwhelmed our frontier police force, which originally, accepted and discharged all facets of policing in the west. No matter what the request from Ottawa, members accepted the task and usually carried it out successfully. "Never say No!" was the philosophy. The job was undertaken without question and every effort was made to meet the challenges, no matter the burden.

Such was the case when the RCMP expanded from small prairie communities to large cities, beginning with Burnaby in the early 1950s. The staffing logistics were extremely taxing, sapping the force in many other areas. 'Robbing Peter to pay Paul' became policy. Many operations ran shorthanded in an effort to "feed the monster" in southern British Columbia.

Loathe to lobby government for more, administrators attempted to deal with inadequate resource internally. Amazingly, overtime pay wasn't a factor until the late 1970s; members worked extra hours for free, often toiling alongside municipal police who were paid overtime.

As Canada began transitioning to a multicultural society, exacerbated by population growth, more cracks and fissures appeared. The RCMP's basic para-military infrastructure did not change and it continued to be responsible for all levels of policing from coast to coast. Provincial and growing municipal contracts were demanding more resources. Our frontier police force was attempting to be all things to all people in what was becoming a very diversified country.

Trying to balance all this while also handling Canada's national security caused serious shortcomings during the 1960s. The government acted on the McDonald Commission's recommendation and removed security services from the RCMP purview, but the force did not relinquish this responsibility voluntarily. It had to be arbitrarily taken away.

Today, even after the Brown study recommended internal changes, few upper echelon RCMP executives or politicians focus on the essential problem – multi-jurisdictional saturation.

Management makes lofty policy statements about elevating professionalism, improving the management environment and urging members to "meet the challenge." Detachments operate under strength daily. Morale doesn't improve and members feel under siege, both inwardly and outwardly.

Sadly, the force seems headed for the cliff. Like the emperor without clothes, the problem of 'mandate overload' is massive and should be obvious, yet not a single voice speaks up.

The time has come to admit that the RCMP can no longer attempt to be all things to all people.

The RCMP has so many diversified and complex tasks, at so many levels, that the appearance of success is becoming more and more elusive. Immediate action must be taken to bring it into the 21st century. It must be extricated from municipal and provincial contracts – provincial contracts are up for renewal in 2012 – and transition to an exclusively federal focus.

The Force must concentrate its considerable expertise on federal responsibilities. It could be deployed in an ASSISTANCE capacity when asked to help provincial and municipal agencies involving serious and/or interprovincial crime.

Rather than being distracted by a myriad of assorted demands, the force could target national maladies such as biker gangs, terrorism, corporate and economic crime and other national criminal maladies. Through mandate transition, there may still be time to prevent this noble "herd" from plunging over the cliff.

It will be a psychological debilitating national trauma if the 'RCMP herd' is not turned around and saved from destruction. Our leaders have a responsibility to ensure that this national treasure, a Canadian icon etched indelibly into our psyche, is preserved. The RCMP is still admired worldwide and Canada will be a smaller country without it.

Turning the herd will not be easy. There will be resistance at all levels. The logistics are difficult and complex. Resistance to change will be rampant. It will take great political courage and dynamic leadership.

If current leaders do not display courage and stamina and move on these initiatives, the RCMP will continue to be deluged with a complexity of problems from the multi-levels of jurisdiction it now futilely wrestles with. The disasters will continue. It will sadly be swallowed up by a barrage of criticism and find itself broken and dying at the bottom of the cliff.

Author: Retired S/Sgt. Ian Parsons

CHAPTER #13

Extra Ordinary Duty

» » Pass the Buck » »

We were responding to a call of a person who had collapsed in an elevator of an old hotel in Kamloops. Upon arrival it was noted that this person was terribly obese, and after collapsing in this small elevator I could see that two members would have a considerable amount of hassle getting the subject removed. My partner came to the rescue noticing this subject was moaning. He was sharp enough to remark that he thought the subject was mumbling something about back problems. With that clue, I immediately had the hotel attendant call for an ambulance. Both of us then stood back and watched ambulance attendants struggle for at least 20 minutes with this subject. This female subject was taken to the local hospital strapped to a stretcher where the doctor on call merely diagnosed her as being overly drunk. Our dilemma was not over as this person carried probably 300 lbs and was dead weight. We had to remove her back to our cells. I managed to convince the staff at the hospital that the subject should remain strapped in the stretcher while we transport her back to the Detachment. Delivery was made with me riding in the back of the prisoner van to ensure she didn't fall off. After rolling the medical stretcher into the drunk tank it was only a matter of lowering the stretcher to the lowest possible level and rolling her off and into a prone position. We followed protocol to ensure our prisoner was safe to remove to cells. We were glad medical professionals at the hospital checked on her condition before bringing her back to the drunk tank. We never did clue the ambulance attendants in on our ploy that night.

» »   Checking Americans   » »

I worked with an African American auxiliary member who joined us on patrol occasionally. If we checked American tourists travelling through town on the Trans Canada Highway, he enjoyed lighting up his cigar and then take particular pleasure in approaching the driver. He would use his southern drawl, and ask "You -all gonna be in Canada for a long time?"

» »   Giving directions   » »

It was funny to pick the right time to confuse some poor individual who was looking for directions to get to a particular part of town. I would start by saying" You gotta go 3 blocks north, no that's blocked off, you have to go down the street and through a set of lights and then turn left. Sorry that's a one way street. Try heading south on that street and come around by taking that street, Oh I forgot that's under construction. "I'm sorry sir, you can't get there from here". It was priceless to see the bewildered look on his face. At this point, I would apologize and tell him where to go. I'm sure a few left thinking I was ready for a relaxing vacation somewhere.

» »   Dog sled vs Skidoo   » »

While at Fort Chipewyan Detachment I made a skidoo trip south to touch base with local trappers along the river. Sometimes I would carry a message or some mail for them. The skidoo would clip along nicely on the beaten track used by sled dogs along the river bank. I nearly had a head- on collision with one trapper and his team. As both of us stopped to chat, the decision was made to stop and have tea, allowing the dogs to rest at the same time. The trapper made a small fire, brewed some tea and shared some bannock with me as we visited.

As we packed up the gear, I made a bet with the trapper that he might even beat me home that day. The trapper commenced to go to each dog he had already harnessed up and pulled an imaginary starter cord at the neck of each dog in the same fashion I had started my skidoo. I know he was telling me that his equipment would outlast mine any day, so I wished him well as my patrol continued.

» » Wolf tracks » »

It was enjoyable being stationed in a location where you had such varied duties throughout the year. This two man detachment had several pieces of equipment we had to work with including a 4x4 International panel truck; a snow coach made by bombardier; a 25 ft. deep V twin engine patrol boat. I also used my own private skidoo for some patrols however we used the local bush pilot for a lot of work. The many trips I did make with this bush pilot on his routine mail runs took me to various outposts within the detachment area. I remember those moments in spring when we were called upon by the Parks Department to chase the buffalo away from the Catfish River and try to herd them further back to the Wood Buffalo Park grasslands. I actually took 8 mm movie of some of those patrols. I recall flying with George Hart one day and responding without thought to his question: "Did you see those wolf tracks down there?" At 1500 to 2000 feet, I like a dummy said "Where"? That was his cue to lower the boom and take a nose dive with his Sessna 185 aircraft to an area covered in shrubs and tall grass. It scared the hell out of me, and after he levelled the plane off, he would laugh and ask me again "Did you see them?" Of course I did.

» » Mercy Flight to Fort McMurray » »

In northern remote postings, local bush pilots were sometimes called upon to make an emergency medical evacuation flight to a larger city to get very ill patients to hospital. These were sometimes referred to as "Mercy Flights". Decisions were sometimes made to fly under very poor weather conditions. It was late fall and the air was chilly. One close call related to a mercy flight to Fort McMurray which could have turned to near tragedy as George Hart, the bush pilot, told me later. A lady who had been beaten and raped was being transported to Fort McMurray hospital. I went along with the local nurse to accompany the flight. Just before dark, the Cessna 185 float plane took off from a small lake just out of Fort Chipewyan and unknown to me at the time, the planes pontoons narrowly missed the trees at the end of the lake. The two hour flight would put us into Fort McMurray just before 10:30 p.m., but how does one land on a river at night with a float plane? Advance notice was given to Fort McMurray Detachment to divert and direct as many vehicles from the main street and line them up on the riverbank with headlights shinning across the river channel. This would give George a better look a the surface of the water. It was neat to see that there were many vehicles parked along the river's edge giving sufficient light to allow for a safe landing.

George made a pass allowing the pontoons to just touch the surface of the water on the river channel to create more ripple. The second pass allowed for a smooth touchdown. The doctor met us at the river's edge only to pronounce the women we had on board 'dead' on arrival. I knew then I had become more deeply involved in the case as it turned into a murder file.

» » **Mercy Flight turned fatal** » »

It didn't seem right that, after all those experiences, one had to go through the unpleasant task of protecting the scene of a plane crash where George Hart, the pilot I had flown with so many times, and 4 others perished. He was on another one of those mercy flights taking sick patients from Fort Chipewyan to Fort Smith, NWT. The weather conditions were poor that winter and George had experience in flying during that kind of weather. This time it was not to be.

He flew into a whiteout and put his plane into the frozen lakebed not 10 miles from the Detachment. The frozen lakebed lay quiet, holding what was left of a Cessna 185 in a wreckage that could have been trucked away in a 3/4 ton pickup. George remains in my memory as one of those unsung heroes we all become accustomed to when living in remote communities in the north.

While assisting the transport investigators at the plane crash scene, I vividly recall working with them to determine which part of the plane made contact with the frozen lakebed. It quickly became apparent that the plane flew almost directly downward and at a slight angle just before it made contact. Investigators concluded that this pilot may have been used to only flying with his trust in visual surroundings, as opposed to trusting his instruments.

As we were slowly recovering pieces of debris on site, I realized that all the people who were on this flight had perished probably did not suffer in their deaths. I remember recovering a wallet from the back left pant pocket where the pilot seat and lower torso was still in tact. It was still stuffed with hundreds of dollars the pilot was carrying. Everything else from the deceased body from the belt line up was missing. The upper torso had disintegrated on impact. Moments later, the only thing that I discovered was the bridge of the pilot's nose laying in the snow that reminded me of the pilot I had flown with so many times before.

Upon reflecting back on that day, I recall the two nursing station nurses discussing who should accompany the patients on that fateful flight. They flipped a coin and only one could go. Julie King won the coin toss. Mary Rafter, the other nurse learned of her partner's fate hours later when the plane was reported missing.

» » **Leave it to Beaver** » »

A junior constable responds to a complaint on an interior of British Columbia reserve with an unusual task. Apparently a "rabid" beaver was on the loose causing havoc to the local residence. The beaver was reported as chasing subjects if they came too close. After a short patrol the constable spots the suspect along the roadway beside the river. He describes the animal as a rather large looking beaver with large teeth.

He approached the animal with caution in an attempt to see if the allegations were really true. Sure enough, the beaver challenged and started chasing the constable back towards the police car. During the retreat the constable had no time to open the police car door and merely took retreat on top of the hood of the police transport. After summoning help, the only embarrassing comment that came from the investigating members was "Boy could that beaver run, I've never seen a beaver move so fast!" Needless to say, the talk amongst the boys back at the office covered a number of different twists concerning this member's ability to handle a beaver.

» » Counting Eagles » »

While stationed in northern BC during the 1950's I recall we had to submit monthly reports through proper channels on how many eagles we had seen during the month. I guess during that time some organization was interested in north American numbers for the species. It seemed ridiculous that we would have to submit such a report amongst our other duties.

» » Dog Control » »

I was posted in a northern community dealing with 4 small First Nations Reserves. I was on days off when I was called in to assist other members as they were called by CFS (Community & Family Services), to remove a 3 year-old child from a home. The members required my assistance with dealing with two large pit-bull dogs, as they were mean and I had experience in dealing with such dogs. I bought some cheese and cracker packages from the local store to help me with keeping the dogs occupied while the authorities would be dealing with the adults and conducting their duties in removing the child from this home.

Upon arrival, the CFS authorities asked me to take the 3 year-old boy out into the garage with the two pit-bull dogs. They expected me to keep the dogs and the child occupied while they spoke with the mother and other adults in the home. Here was my chance to put my skills to work in keeping the dogs occupied. I thought it would be nice to have the 3 year old help me give some cheese and crackers to the dogs so I commenced to partially open each package and give it to the three year-old.

The entire reason why we were there in the first place suddenly occurred to me as I watched the 3 year old start eating the cheese and crackers as if he had not eaten in days.

Even the dogs were getting a little frustrated wondering why they were not getting any. It was challenging to keep all things under control without getting the dogs agitated, so I let the little guy gulp down what I had with just a few crumbs for the dogs to sniff and clean up. The three year old was taken from the home without incident.

» » Facing Death in Bosnia » »

I recall Terry Pukas coming back from Bosnia and relating his story. I really think that Bosnia, as well as the following train incident, somehow changed Terry. For good or bad I'm not sure, but something about the man was different. Terry was on a tour of duty in Bosnia, on a Peace Keeping Mission. He had taken leave from his UN job and was traveling to the Ukraine to visit relatives still in the old country. On his return trip to Bosnia, the train he was on was suddenly stopped in the middle of the night in Serbian held territory. Police came through each car taking the odd person off the train. In Terry's car they came up to him after looking everyone over and told him to get off the train.

He was the only person removed from his car. Once outside they questioned him in regards to who he was, what he was up to, obviously looking for the enemy amongst the passengers. They would not believe him that he was with the UN, and accused him of being an enemy soldier. Terry stated over and over who he was, that he was there to help "both sides" and was impartial. The more he spoke the more enraged the person questioning him became. The man, while screaming, suddenly removed his pistol from his holster and put it to Terry's head. Terry said the guy had totally gone berserk and was getting ready to pull the trigger. Terry said he knew he was going to be shot, no question about it, and was praying hard. Suddenly another policeman came up to the one with the pistol and essentially said he could not just shoot the person right there beside the train with all the witnesses looking out the windows at them. The one with the gun hesitated and finally, in a rage, put his gun away and they let him re-board the train.

Terry knew that without the intervention of the second officer he would definitely have been shot. The guy who had the gun to his head had totally lost it, and was practically foaming at the mouth. Needless to say he was very fortunate and couldn't get on the train fast enough. Sadly, Terry developed cancer shortly thereafter. He steadfastly believed his cancer was from the spent munitions such as uranium depleted antitank rounds that were everywhere over there. I do know that Terry cared deeply about the Force, his family and life in general. He had a zest for life I have never seen before or since. Maybe his faith in God did save him that night, and I guess Terry knew that for sure.

» » Dog Packs in Kosovo » »

In late September, 2000, I was about six weeks into my new job as an instructor at the Kosovo Police Service School in Vushtrii, Kosovo, about thirty k.m. north of Prishtina. I was one of ten retired RCMP members assigned to the school under contract to the Organization for Security Coordination in Europe (OSCE) to assist in building a new police service for Kosovo. In order to provide perspective on our situation, it should be mentioned that there were approximately 220 international instructors at the school from twenty-four donor countries. At this time, there were also approximately 100 Canadian police officers from the RCMP and a number of city and municipal police forces across Canada who were assigned to the United Nations Mission in Kosovo (UNMIK) Police.

Many of them were posted to UN Headquarters in Prishtina, detachments in the Prishtina area and other population centers throughout Kosovo, also with many police officers from a number of other participating countries.

It was more than a year since the end of the NATO bombing campaign to drive out Milosevich's Yugoslav Army and the end of his attempt to expel the Albanian speaking Kosovars, the majority ethnic population of the province. Although Kosovo was now being governed under UN mandate, and goods were starting to appear in the markets, conditions were still far from normal. There was garbage everywhere, roads and streets were badly potholed and most of the social and business infrastructure needed rebuilding.

In addition to the human tragedy and misery caused by war, there is another related dimension. What happens to domestic animals, especially dogs, which under normal conditions are so dependent on their special relationship with humans? When abandoned by their masters, dogs revert to the wolf-pack mentality. So it was that in Prishtina and outlying rural areas, there were numerous packs of twelve to thirty dogs, of many breeds and descriptions, trailing through the streets and fields in search of food, howling, barking and fighting through the night. I had seen this before, in West Beirut, during the 1982/84 period, where the dogs had to finally be dispatched by the security forces and militias. In Kosovo, this was the responsibility of the NATO patrols, which covered population areas in support of the UNMIK Police. It seemed that NATO would clear a dog-pack from an area and not many days later another pack would arrive to take its place.

During my first few weeks in Kosovo, I shared a billet with three other RCMP retirees in the Dragadon District, a residential area on a steep side-hill rising several hundred feet westward from Prishtina town centre. While here, several times I saw dog-packs led by large, white, wolf-like animals with heavy mane-like fur on the backs of their necks.

They actually had a magnificent appearance and I thought they could have, quite recently, descended from a breed of Balkan wolves. They reminded me of the wolves drawn by Al Capp when he featured the Wolf Gal in his old comic strip, "Lil Abner".

Now, back to late September. I had recently moved from the Dragadon to an accommodation on the other side of Prishtina. It was my birthday and I had agreed to celebrate it with my ex-RCMP buddies, Larry Ellis, Gene Slobod and Ford Matchim, who were still at the Dragadon billet. So, I walked up the hill to their house and enjoyed some rum and coke. At about 9:45 p.m., I had just left their house and was walking home, downhill, when I was beset by three of these huge white creatures, which seemed to have come out of nowhere.

They barked and snarled ferociously and formed an arc about ten feet in front of me. I had no means of defense (the OSCE did not want its employees armed) and I was caught in the open street with no place to run. I faced them and concentrated on growling (and screaming) louder than they were. This continued for about twenty seconds with no sign of assistance from nearby houses. Over my shoulder, I caught sight of the headlights of a vehicle turning up the Dragadon from the base of the hill. As the vehicle grew nearer, the beasts suddenly retreated and quickly disappeared. I motioned the vehicle to a stop, noting it was from the UNMIK Police and that the lone driver had a Saskatoon Police Department shoulder flash on his uniform. We joked. I informed him that he had probably just saved me from being torn to shreds. He said, "yeah, NATO's supposed to be shooting them". I retorted "They're not doing it fast enough".

During my previous foreign postings and during service in Canada, I had a number of scary experiences, but I cannot remember ever being so startled as when I was beset by the dogs in Kosovo. While on detachment in Canada, I had seen photos of the mangled remains of a victim of an attack by sled dogs. At the time, I remember thinking "any other way but this". Oddly, I never heard of any other mission members, many of whom lived on the Dragadon hill, having a similar experience. Also, I did not hear of any of the local population, particularly children, being attacked by the dogs. Maybe the constant threat of the NATO patrols had an effect.

The next day, while at the police school, I mentioned the incident to Larry and Gene. I couldn't help but note a degree of skepticism while the conversation turned to the number of rum and cokes we'd had the evening before. John Toews - 2004

CHAPTER #14

Quotes On Assessments

Performance assessments are a fact of life within any policing organization. Most supervisors would not have difficulty writing positive comments on how well a member was performing in their duties. The challenge would come when something adverse or negative had to be said about past performance.

» » **Square peg in a round hole** » »

The following quote was written by a senior supervisor who was reviewing a lengthy report submitted by a trainer and Training Supervisor on a member who was not meeting the standard of performance to pass the Recruit Field Training Program. He had been placed on extension and was on stress leave awaiting a decision by upper management on whether to process the member as a failure with intention to discharge. The senior supervisor quotes "This constable is a prime example of the Force trying to fit a square peg into a round hole."

» » **Quotes From Federal Employee files** » »

The following is a list of quotes from Government Employee Assessments. This has been shared with a few supervisors who would get a chuckle out of them and make the odd statement that they have the odd individual under their command who comes close to fitting the descriptions given. I have shared this list with many Training Officers during Field Training Officer Courses I have delivered.

"Since my last report, he has reached rock bottom and has started to dig."

"His men would follow him anywhere, but only out of morbid curiosity."

"I would not allow this employee to breed."

"This employee is really not so much of a has-been, but more of a definitely won't be."

"Works well when under constant supervision and cornered like a rat in a trap."

"When she opens her mouth, it seems that this is only to change whichever foot was previously in there."

"He would be out of his depth in a parking lot puddle."

"This young lady has delusions of adequacy."

"She sets low personal standards, and then consistently fails to achieve them."

"This employee should go far and the sooner he starts, the better.

"This employee is depriving a village somewhere of an idiot."

"No one can be absolutely useless - One can always be used as a horrible example"

CHAPTER #15

On Patrol

» » Accepting Gratuities » »

There was nothing more difficult than to deal with a local merchant (restaurant manager) who wanted to give you a free meal or coffee and doughnuts just out of gratitude for showing up and having a police presence in his establishment. We were taught not to accept gratuities from individuals as some day we may have to come back and investigate something involving that person. I finally learned to save face with the merchant who would push the point and put the money back in my hand telling me to leave and that it was O.K. The rest of the patrons would turn their heads to see what I would do. I finally succeeded in shoving the money back and not asking for change. I would simply indicate the money was left as a tip to the person who served us. Sufficient money was left to cover the cost of the food purchased.

» » Have you got your other pants? » »

I used to enjoy stopping motorists and upon approaching the lone driver of the vehicle would ask. "Have you got your other pants with you today sir?" The driver of the vehicle would look bewildered at my question, until I explained: "The reason I said this is that the last few vehicles I had checked, all the drivers said they left their drivers licences' in their other pants".

»» Free 24 hour suspension »»

During the latter part of my career I got a kick out of the reactions from people I would give my calling card to, when I would write on the back of the card *one free 24 hour suspension* or *one get out of jail free*. You would be surprised how many people would come up to me years later stating they still had the card in their wallet in case they needed it. I keep waiting for the phone to ring and have some member ask me what I was trying to prove with what was written on the back of the calling cards.

»» You're living with the Creep »»

For those of us who recall being complaint takers there are key incidents that stand out. One I recall vividly was when I observed a colleague of mine taking a call from what I assumed was a distraught women making a complaint about her husband or a significant other. I remember this member kept asking the caller "What's your name?" After a few moments I heard him reply "Well, you're living with the creep!" and then he hung up. In today's policing environment a lot more steps are taken to ensure police look into such calls and help victims of abuse. Today at least, there are methods of handling calls like that to assist the public with a follow-up by Victim Services volunteers.

»» Overdue Trapper »»

It's Christmas Eve in Fort Chipewyan Alberta, and from one family in this remote northern community comes a cry for help. A trapper was expected home the night before with his dog team.

Our information was that the bush pilot saw the trapper on Athebasca Lake in the late daylight hours heading for home with his dog team. By this time it was expected that he would be close to the community but concerns were still there.

It was time for some action so arrangements were made to put some men out on snowmobiles to take a trip up the lake on the common trail used for trappers and try to locate our subject. The wind was picking up, and while it was a clear night, the blowing snow left visibility to less than a 1/4 mile. We started out using the dog trail as our guide and had the snowmobiles spread out far enough so they could see each other as we went up the lake. Not a few miles out of town we met up with the dog team and sled which appeared to be packed, but.. no rider?

The sleigh came to a stop and the dogs appeared exhausted. Their tongues hanging out as if to be pleased to have a breather. Their faces were full of ice crystals from the blowing snow. A moment later blankets from the sled were tossed aside and out came the man we were looking for. He had stopped earlier in the day to make tea and rest the dogs giving good reason for being late from the original schedule. He was glad that we had taken the steps to check on his well-being.

On the return home I had the misfortune of not keeping close enough watch on the lake's ice surface, where scale ice was protruding causing a shelving effect with different sheets of ice. The left front ski on my snowmobile had gone underneath and from impact was completely sheared off. I could see the lights from Fort Chipewyan in a distance and knew that home base was not far away. The rest of the group slowed down enough allowing me to limp home on one ski. I would have to place all my body weight leaning heavily to the right side of the snowmobile to ensure limited damage to the front end ski equipment.

» » **Dropping your gun** » »

Over the years there have been many changes to the uniform. The 'Sam Brown' equipment we used up to now had some flaws that required immediate reporting to material management, if the equipment malfunctioned. I recall working midnight shift on some back street near the main highway leading out of town. It was close to midnight and raining enough for me to wear my raincoat. While I was checking one transient, my Sam Brown holster, which carried my gun, fell to the ground from underneath the raincoat. My professional image dropped a few points just then. The subject I checked left laughing to himself. As I collected my swallowed pride, I picked up the holster with its weapon, and left as quickly as I could.

»» Cards anyone? »»

I recall working as a plainclothes officer one evening. We were on a stakeout watching a target of interest and time was dragging on. My partner and I were at our wit's end about what we could do to keep ourselves occupied while waiting for something to happen.

Suddenly I notice my partner starts tearing pages from his note book and writing on them. I asked him what he was doing. I soon noted that he was making up a deck of cards. The rest of the shift went quickly.

»» Passing the Time »»

Whenever we were called for special duty it was always - 'hurry up and wait'. On this one occasion a busload of us had to leave quite early and head for a specific area because of a road block in the interior of B.C. Things were somewhat tense because we were told people at the blockade had weapons and were not in the mood for negotiating. After getting into position for the night, duties were assigned to various groups of members depending on the degree of security that was needed on the back roads leading to this blockade.

Nobody thought about bringing a deck of cards or some other game to keep us occupied while we were waiting for further instructions. Hours past and finally one of the guys came up with this idea. He took a Styrofoam cup, made the rim wet, and placed a single sheet of Kleenex tissue on the top of the cup. In the middle he placed a dime and set the rules. Four or five could play the game and to the winner went 25 cents. Each had to put 25 cents into the cup at the beginning of the game. We used a cigarette to start burning holes in the single sheet of tissue until the dime fell into the cup. Each took his turn and the group had to agree that a burn was complete when you saw the tissue actually glow. The trick was to ensure that the cigarette was free from ashes so one would blow at it to make sure he had a neat hot tip to work with. We went through a few cigarettes alright, but it sure passed the time.

» » Carry On! » »

Routine Patrol, Steveston, B.C. It was a hot summer night and around 04:00 hrs when I approached an older model Maverick 4 door sedan parked along the south dyke by the Fraser River. I pulled up about 30 to 40 feet behind the car. It appeared vacant. I looked around, nobody on the dyke. I then flashed my high beams and still no response.

As I approached the vehicle I noticed the windows were down and I couldn't see or hear anything. As I got closer I observed several items laying on the rear window ledge. Much to my surprise there was an open 1/2 full jar of Vaseline, a set of dentures, and an 8 to 10" portion of Kielbasa Ukrainian Sausage. Once beside the vehicle I observed two occupants, stark naked in the rear seat.

They were both about 50 years old, and didn't appear startled or upset with my presence. I asked if everything was O.K? The man replied "Oh yes officer, we're just a couple of middle aged folks having a good time." The female smiled and nodded. I said "Carry On" and departed.

» » Back to the Fort » »

After spending a few weeks at Fort McMurray, Alta in the Fall of 1968 it was nice once in a while to take the P.C. and head out of town to blow the rust out of the carburetor. The Alberta Oil Sands project was just getting underway. I took this opportunity one morning and found the trip towards the airport most interesting. The highway was still being constructed to accommodate the heavy traffic during the boom and with the spring thaw underway a number of frost boils were fun to avoid on the road. I missed several, however caught one with sufficient force to create damage to the exhaust system underneath the P.C.

I checked things out and found that the front exhaust pipe had snapped just at the back of the muffler and was hanging down in such a way as to not allow me to continue driving forward.

I tried to dispatch for a tow truck however one was not immediately available. What the heck, I was only about 3 miles out of town.

It's emergency lights time, and I drive in reverse all the way to the first service station for repairs. I got a few good looks from the locals as the sparks were flying underneath the P.C. It's amazing how sore your neck gets when you continuously drive looking backwards for some distance.

» » Dumpster Intelligence » »

You know nothing good will come out of a story that started with, "So I met this guy in the dumpster". When I worked general duties in Whalley, I had an intelligence file that came in with that exact storyline.

The complainant supposedly met another guy when rooting through the same dumpster accidentally. The one guy asked my complainant if he wanted to buy a car. He's in a dumpster for Christ sake. He was offered it for a little money in return. The complainant asked the fellow why it was so cheap and the guy said it was stolen. I followed up on this, and despite how absurd it sounded, found the house the complainant said the car would be at. Believe it or not, the car was actually reported stolen! I recovered it. The complainant came back wanting money for this info, but I never gave him any.

» » Stolen Guitar » »

I attended a call where two guys were in some sort of fight, and while it was going on, one of the participants had his guitar stolen. Upon attending to this complaint I took the details and sent the two combatants on their way. A short time later I noted an individual sitting in a drunken stupor on the street and decided to pick the person up for being drunk in public. Something caught my eye as this person had with him a guitar that did not seem to fit the picture. Sure enough, after looking into why he had possession of the guitar, I had sufficient evidence to charge the individual with possession of stolen property. I guess I hit two birds with one stone.

» » Suicide Call Victim » »

We got a call that a man had shot himself and it took us almost an hour to get to the location of where the incident occurred in Southern Manitoba. Upon arrival I noted a male lying on the ground with a 22 calibre rifle between his legs. There was a bullet hole in the bottom of his chin and blood coming from his mouth. He had been in this position for at least an hour according to witnesses.

My partner and I started taking notes from witnesses and actually taking statements as to who discovered the body, etc. After about ½ hour of this, something told me to maybe go back and actually check the victim to confirm that he was dead.

Sure enough, I check his pulse and he has a strong heart beat. I alerted my partner that the victim is still alive and that we should get him to the doctor ASAP. The problem was, if we called for an ambulance, that would take at least 40 minutes for them to arrive and another 40 to get the victim to the doctor. We both decided to take the victim with the police transport directly to the Doctor. We loaded the victim in a prone position across the back seat of the police car and made sure that he was not choking on any blood that was coming from his mouth.

I drove the police car to the max down that highway thinking there was a chance we could save the individual. My partner was in the front seat making sure that an extra set of eyes were on the road as I was pushing the police transport to the limit.

As I was focusing on my driving skills I was not paying that much attention to our victim. I could not believe my eyes when I saw the victim sit up in the back seat and start trying to say something. Because the bullet had gone through his tongue, it became swollen to the point that the victim could not properly speak. It was something that you see in a horror movie. I thought the guy was near dead.

Upon arrival at the doctor's office, the doctor examined the victim and was able to remove a .22 calibre led bullet from the roof of the victim's mouth with a pair of forceps. The victim was released from the hospital the next day.

» » Too funny to charge » »

I stopped an impaired driver near Verdon, Manitoba years ago. The 73 yr- old man was all over the road at 4:00 a.m. As the subject tried to find his driver's licence in his wallet, all of the cards and documents stored in the wallet just blew up in front of him like a deck of cards that spring out of your hands. The subject then proceeded to bend over towards his immediate right to try and attempt to retrieve his drivers licence that fell to the floor. Several moments past and all I could see was the crack of his bum and his pants almost falling off as he leaned over to find his documents.

The smell of alcoholic liquor was evident, giving me reasonable and probable grounds to believe he was impaired. Moments past, with little or no activity other than what appeared to be an eternity for this man trying to find his driver's license. All of a sudden, his left hand came out from the darkness under the seat of the car and in it was a social insurance card. It appeared the suspect was trying to hand this document to me. I retrieved it from his hand and discovered it to be a social insurance card. I proceeded to inform the man that this was not his driver's licence but was his social insurance card. He quickly replied, while still continuing to be bent over looking for his documents, "That's O.K., I thought I would give you something to read while you wait."

This blew me away, to the point that I started laughing and found the response most amusing. I made the decision to take the man home to his wife. - No charges.

» »   I killed that guy!   » »

Snow Lake Manitoba: I get a call from the Detachment Commander that I have a two day old murder to investigate. Word came in via the forestry fire towers that are located throughout the area. The initial information was sketchy as radio transmissions from one fire tower to the other were simple and to the point.

I had to plan my trip into a remote area with all the gear and tools to conduct an investigation, not knowing what to expect. In these parts, there are no specialized groups to follow you into the scene and take over. I had about a 20 mile trip across the lake and up a waterway to reach my location. I arrived at the camp I was looking for in the early evening and was met by a First Nations male at the dock.

With little communication started, this adult male states "I killed that guy!" I am just starting to get settled on getting onto the dock and was shocked at this first bit of information gleaned. In an attempt to gather a better handle of what happened I replied to this man, "How come did you do it?" His quick reply was "He pissed me off!". I sized up this individual and found him to be a reasonable man coming forward to assist me in the docking. I took the position of making things a little light and said to him "I will try really hard while I am here not to piss you off", to which the accused started laughing aloud. I made no arrest at this point and went towards the area with this man where it was learned the body was located. What I found was a deceased male who had been covered with a blanket and who had been beaten to death with a club instrument. His face was a total mess.

At initial examination of the scene, the accused casually points out to me that the chunk of wood he used for the beating was still where he had left it not far from the body. He stated he left it there because he thought the police would need it. What I found so astounding was that these people were so honest about their behaviour that there was little or no element of deception. They certainly know how to break the law, however later they were very accommodating to the process of police following up on an investigation. I found this to be quite unique, as a quality I admired amongst the people I had encountered.

»» Not My Day »»

I checked a guy one day with a wife and kid in the car. He had been caught speeding. Upon coming up to the driver's side window, I noted that the driver (husband) had just rolled down his window and this god awful smell began emitting from the vehicle. This man's young infant had apparently soiled himself in the car. The infant had recently puked all over the front seat of the car. The smell was something that hit me with a shock. To top it off, I noted that his wife was on his case giving him hell for getting caught speeding.

This man's first comment to me after asking for driver's license was "This is definitely not my day". My immediate reaction was, this poor man has enough coming at him, he does not need this traffic ticket to add to his day. I just stated words to the effect, "Sir, you just move along, you have enough on your plate today." I felt sorry for both him and his wife.

»» All fired up »»

In 2001, while on shift in Alberta, I was dispatched to investigate a complaint of someone torching a vehicle at a certain location. We had a good idea who our suspect was because he had a reputation of doing this in the area. Sure enough, I found our suspect and arrested him. The trouble was he had little or no hands to speak of, because he had burnt them years ago setting fires. It was near to impossible to handcuff this guy as they would slip off when you tried to put them on. I put him in the police transport and started driving back to the Detachment. I could smell the smoke from the burning car on my uniform as we were travelling, not thinking that what was really going on was that my suspect had started a fire inside the back seat of the police transport.

Upon looking back all I could see was flames all over the back seat. My suspect had his feet up against the silent patrolman, which is the protective shield installed just behind the front bench seat.

After stopping and getting the suspect out of the back seat, all I could do was stand back and watch my patrol vehicle go up in flames in front of me. What some cops won't do to get a new police transport for the Detachment.

»» Putting her at ease ««

My recruit and I were heading out on a 911 call to the Reserve dealing with some sort of incident that made my recruit a little nervous. As we were driving down the road we were talking about what kinds of things we should be ready for. I could see that my recruit was getting a little up tight as we were getting closer to our intended location. She asked what might happen and I quickly tried to put her at ease with some light humour by remarking - "If I don't make it, you can have my big screen TV, and if you don't make it, I want your fridge." The look on her face was priceless.

»» Tough tow job ««

I was posted in Fort St. John, B.C. at the time. I attended a motor vehicle accident where a BC Telephone vehicle had gone off the road and down a steep embankment about 100 feet. The BC Tel vehicle had hit a tree on the way down the embankment which was the only thing that prevented the vehicle from continuing another several hundred feet down. The driver was taken to hospital by Emergency Health Services people. The vehicle had sustained some front end damage from the tree, but was repairable. The wrecker attended and I had to block the road as the tow truck owner/operator was attempting to recover the vehicle.

It became obvious that the tow truck was not powerful enough to recover the vehicle. As the winch strained to pull the vehicle up the hill, the tow truck would climb the chalk blocks, until the driver would release the winch. After watching this for some time, I approached the tow truck driver and told him I was calling another wrecker with a larger, more powerful truck. He said that he was the wrecker on call for the week, and he would make the recovery. Fort St. John had 3 wrecking companies, each had a week to be the police on call wrecker. I watched for a while longer as the same fruitless effort continued with this underpowered tow truck.

I had finally run out of time and patience. There was a BC Tel employee also waiting for this recovery so that he could retrieve the expensive equipment that was still in the vehicle. I was approaching the tow truck again to tell the tow truck operator that I was calling a bigger truck. As I approached the tow truck, it jumped the chalk blocks. I was right at the tow truck driver's door at this time, so I jumped in the truck, thinking I could hit the brakes and stop the truck from going down the embankment as well. I was wrong! I jumped in the driver's seat, applied the brake with all my might. The four tires were locked up, but skidding as the BC Tel vehicle was sliding back down the hill, pulling the tow truck with it. Next thing I know, I am in the driver's seat of a tow truck, going down a steep embankment, backwards! The BC Tel employee who was at the scene said to me, "I thought you were looking through binoculars, your eyes were so big".

As luck would have it, the BC Tel vehicle hit the same tree again stopping it from continuing down the embankment. I, in the tow truck bounced high enough to land on top of the BC Tel vehicle, and also hit the tree.

The tree saved me from going several hundred feet down the hill too, but was now bowing with the wait of the two vehicles against it. I scurried out of the tow truck as fast as I could, and back up to the top of the hill.

A bigger tow truck did in fact come to the scene, to recover the original tow truck, and the BC Tel vehicle. Meanwhile, I was instructed to complete another accident report. This report had me as the *driver* of the tow truck. The damage column of the BC Tel vehicle on this accident report read, "totally destroyed, unrepairable".

» » Best Customer » »

I was stationed in Prince Rupert from July 1972 to August of 1976. I'm 6'2' and I was one of the smaller members on the shift I was assigned.

Mr. Horn Wong, a Chinese gentleman owned a clothing store "Fashion Tailors" and had the contract to do alterations to members' uniforms. After a busy weekend of fighting drunks, I took two pairs of long blue uniform pants in to have the damage repaired and this was the first time I met Horn.

He came from the back of his business holding up a pair of another member's long blues. This member was a pretty big guy. Horn was holding the pants as high as he could and was looking through the crotch at me and the legs were still dragging on the floor.

I did my four years in Rupert and went back a year later & dropped in to see Horn. He poured me a small drink of scotch & we talked about the old days. He gave me the ultimate compliment saying I was one of his best customers as almost every Monday I was in with a pair of blues or a shirt that needed repair.

» » That's My Dad » »

I had to do a small school talk at an elementary school one day. I thought I would be unique and brought a few things along for a short 'show and tell' in class. The usual equipment was produced with all kinds of typical questions that come from these kids. I took the liberty to show a few random pictures of individuals that the police have to deal with and explained that sometimes these people have to go to jail or words to that effect. After showing a mug shot or two, one youngster in the class perks up quickly with a remark ' Hey, that's a picture of my dad!". You have to be careful what you take for props to a school talk.

» » The Pigs are here! » »

A few years ago some of us were charged with the responsibility of serving summonses for the Court Detail office. I had to deliver a summons to a subject in the Whalley Flats area of Surrey, B.C. This area of the city was known as the rough part of town. Upon ringing the door bell on Saturday morning, I was met by a youngster, not 5 or 6 yrs old who answered the door and with his face full of food and munching on something, he howlers back towards the kitchen area. "Hey Mom the Fricken Pigs are here!".

The first thing that went through my mind is that I definitely have my work cut out for me for the next 20 years with the attitude this youngster presented at the front door. By the way, I got the summons served.

» » Bad Luck victim » »

Some people have all the bad luck. While working out of Thompson, Manitoba, I had occasion to respond to a call where a fellow had apparently hit a moose on the road. Unfortunately, while en-route to this call, the driver of the victim vehicle was struck by passing traffic at the scene and was killed himself.

» » Lost in the Fog » »

Members stationed in the North West Territories relate a set of events that occurred about 1985 when two members made arrangements for a local charter pilot to fly them to a designated location to follow up on some investigations. The single engine plane would normally file a flight plan on their normal routine. They were expected to make this a reasonably short trip, however once in the air the pilot kept flying into heavier fog and cloudier weather. There was no opportunity for a break in the clouds or the fog to drop down and find their regular landing location. The pilot had concerns about flying too low and perhaps hitting the trees while they were attempting to break through the fog bank. The flight continued with the pilot flying to some degree in circles just to find that break in the clouds. It was not to be.

After prolonged attempts, the young pilot gave up flying in frustration and just put his hands behind his head indicating they were doomed. The one member on the righ-hand seat of the pilot continued to encourage the pilot to keep flying. The second member began getting worried at the crises that had unfolded. He apparently took out his notebook and started writing a final goodbye letter to his loved one, thinking they were going to perish on this flight. It is told that he indicated in his notes 'Sue the bastards!'

The member seated to the right of the pilot noticed a hump in the fog bank off to the right and instructed the pilot to fly in that direction to check it out. He could vaguely see the outline of a hill through the fog and exclaimed that he thought he recognized this landmark as he had been stationed in that area before. At this point it is said that the member either drew his gun or in some way threatened the pilot to continue his flight and to attempt breaking through the fog bank so that they might find a safe landing area. There was concern as to the amount of fuel they might have left. The pilot managed to break through the fog bank near this location and from here continued to fly at low altitudes to find a safe landing location. When they did touch down, it is said that they had limited fuel or were nearly empty on fuel. They were off course by a large margin but safe. After landing, an assault apparently occurred between one of the members and the pilot. Both members were relieved to be on the ground. At this juncture, the pilot offered to fly both members to their original destination when the fog lifted. Needless to say, they refused his offer and took steps to arrange for another plane to come and pick them up.

» »   **Possible Turf thieves**   » »

Some lady called in two nights in a row complaining that she thought there was someone coming through the neighborhood trying to steal pieces of her freshly laid turf on her front lawn. Some strips of turf had been moved sufficiently to suggest that the culprit(s) may have been scared off fearing they might be caught. On the second night however, a closer examination and short surveillance disclosed that a group of raccoons were the culprits. They were in search of grubs that might be located under the turf and quickly moved about lifting the edges of turf to search underneath. No further action taken.

» » Better hurry up » »

In northern Saskatchewan at a remote posting two members of the Force, who had started their shift early, wanted to break for lunch so both decided to go to the local restaurant on the main drag of their community. They knew that if they gulped their lunch down in a hurry they would soon be responding to other calls that needed attention.

While having their meal, a local resident enters the restaurant and tells the two members that he had observed a fight break out just down the street. Both members nodded and indicated they would get to it as soon as they could and continued to eat their meal. After all, the portable radio was close at hand in the event Telecoms requested their assistance.

Moments go by and a second local resident comes into the restaurant approaching the members to advise them that he had seen a fight going on down the street. Again, both members acknowledged the citizen's concern and informed him they were about to head out but were in the process of finishing their meal. The concerned citizen than replied "You had better hurry up, because it looks like one of your buddies in the fight is losing!" After hearing this, both left their respective dinner plates and left the restaurant to come to the aid of their partner in the street.

» » My buddy died » »

Someone came into the office to report one of his buddies had died. I asked how he knew his buddy was dead. Subject replied "I kicked him and he didn't move."

» » Body recovery » »

A call is received in Manitoba that a body had been discovered floating on a remote lake location. Arrangements were made to fly into the lake with a float plane to conduct an investigation. Upon landing and finding the body, it was apparent that no other individuals were in the area. There was no evidence of a boat on the lake.

Investigators had no idea who the deceased was. The body was somewhat decomposed and the pilot of the float plane did not wish to have this body stuffed into the inside of the plane in its current state.

It was decided to tie the body onto the pontoons for transport and continue their investigation once they return back to base. This was done and the flight continued back over rough muskeg terrain. Upon arrival, all that was left on the pontoons were dangling ropes. They had lost the body in flight. It was never learned who the party was.

» » Horsing around » »

During the 1970's, I was on shift when one member of our watch picked up a horse that was found wondering at large outside the local stock yard corrals in Kamloops, B.C. He rode the horse back to the Detachment at about 3:00 a.m. and was making arrangements to get it back to its rightful owner. While waiting, he took the opportunity to ride the horse into the cell block area amongst the sleeping prisoners & turned the horse back out again. I am sure the sound of horse hoofs on the concrete floor woke up a few prisoners. In the morning I was responsible for releasing any prisoners who had stayed the night. The prisoners never said a word next morning. I am sure some had some flashback during the night and perhaps quit drinking as a result.

» » Different perspective » »

I was stationed in Vernon, B.C. after previously doing a stint of duty in Prince Rupert, B.C. While on patrol one night, I noticed a good sized boulder lying on the sidewalk in the business district so I stopped the police car and proceed to pick up the rock with intensions of getting get rid of it.

I had feared that someone might take advantage of it for a smash and grab and did not want to give someone the opportunity to do this. One of my partners drives by and notices me doing this, so he stops to advise that the store owner has used this rock to prop his door open during the day. How your perspective changes on things when you police in different jurisdictions. A rock left on the side walk in Prince Rupert would not have lasted that long. It most certainly would have been used for vandalism or a smash and grab opportunity.

» » Professing her love » »

I got a call of a missing person in Whalley. A girlfriend had reported her boyfriend "missing" as she had not spoken to him for a couple days. I asked her if it was possible that he left her and she told me that she had just taken him on the "Jerry Springer" show to profess her love to him (which she told me she did, by baring her breasts on television, and this woman was about 350 lbs). I ended up calling the boyfriend's family to make sure he wasn't "missing" and the family allowed me to speak with him. He told me that he was horrified that he was on the "Jerry Springer" show with her and that he, indeed, left her. All was well in the end. She did accept the news that he was alive and well and that he just didn't want to talk to her.

» » Stop that truck » »

A Manitoba couple were skipping town without paying rent. They loaded up their truck like the Beverley Hillbillies and off they went. Trouble was, the guy left his truck in neutral causing it to roll backwards. As he tried to jump into the truck and take control, he fell out & got run over, according to witnesses, trying to stop the truck. When I got there I had lots of evidence to charge the guy with impaired driving.

»» You're outa here »»

A fellow living in a trailer park in Surrey, B.C. got tired of one of his neighbors whom he had been having some issues with. One night, after having a few drinks he decided to use his Semi tractor unit to hook up to his neighbor's 35 foot trailer and pull it right off its moorings and out of the trailer park. The couple in the trailer were still sleeping inside the trailer when this occurred. As I am traveling down the King George Highway, I notice this large trailer being pulled out onto the highway, cables and lines still attached. After stopping this Semi unit, I had a good impaired driving charge on my hands. All in all, it was a neat way to get rid of a neighbor.

» » Unusual arrest » »

We entered a residence with a warrant to arrest someone. The subject was deemed a bit of a risk so we were careful and ready in the event he might resist arrest. A few of us checked every room in the home but the suspect was not located. One of the last doors in the house was the bathroom. We opened it with guns drawn and saw our suspect sitting on the can having a dump. We promptly placed him under arrest and his reply was "Let me pinch it off and we'll get going!" - Priceless!!.

» » Impaired case gone bad » »

In the Spring of 1954, I was a member of the Royal Canadian Mounted police who had just about 3 years service and was stationed at Surrey, B.C.. I was working out of the Cloverdale office. My patrol area was all the territory south of the Number 10 Highway all the way to the border and would have included what is now known as the City of White Rock. I was the only guy patrolling this area that chilly Spring evening. I was driving a 1953 Chevy 2 door coupe police vehicle which was black and white and had a large RCMP crest on the door.

I had received a call that a motor vehicle accident had occurred on Semiahmoo Avenue where a vehicle struck 6 other parked cars. Upon arrival I found a male occupant in his vehicle with a heavily damaged front end. With him was a lady, whom I knew was a local prostitute. The driver was obviously drunk and still in his Canada Immigration uniform, yet showing signs of being in shock.

After making initial contact with the driver to see that everyone was O.K., I put the lady from his car into a passing taxi, and went back to deal with the driver. He appeared to be still in some shock so I decided to place him in the passenger side of my police vehicle to keep him comfortable and warm. I left the police car run with the heater on and told him to stay there while I went to conduct my investigation.

As I was collecting information from other sources in the immediate area of the accident scene, a young 10 year old boy came from behind me and tugged at my trouser leg. I thought to myself "what the hell does this young kid want from me?" The boy said "Mister – Mister! Dat man drove away with your car!!" I glanced up the road only to see my police car heading east towards King George Highway. I knew I was in trouble.

I asked if anyone had a car I could borrow to follow. No one came forward other than a man who later told me he was a Saskatchewan farmer. He had a ¾ ton truck and offered his keys to his truck. I told him he would be better off to drive his truck as he knew it better than I did. I jumped into his truck and off we went after the my stolen police car. I temporarily lost sight of the police car and assumed the suspect may have turned right towards the Canada/ USA border as I recalled he was an Immigration Officer. As we approached the border and went through Canada Customs and onto the U.S.A. Customs port, I spotted my stolen police car stopped at the U.S.A. border crossing.

When we approached the car, I jumped out and went in front of the police car with my gun drawn. The driver took one look at me and hit the gas and floored the car taking off quickly, forcing me to jump out of the way. I thought of possibly shooting out one of the tires. I quickly decided this was not a safe maneuver and let him run. It was too dangerous and too close to others who may be hurt from my discharge of the firearm. I watched the police car head south on the Interstate 5 Highway towards Bellingham, Washington.

Back into the truck I jumped and the chase was on at high speeds down the highway. A Washington State Trooper came up behind us with his patrol vehicle and slowed down to stop as we pulled over.

I instructed the farmer to stop his truck and told him to head back to Canada and call the Cloverdale office to inform them of what had happened. I than jumped into the State Troopers police vehicle and told him to pursue the stolen police car which we had lost sight of.

We instructed the Bellingham police to turn on all the red lights at the intersections leading into the city on the highway, which they had the opportunity to control. As we came closer to the city limits I heard one of the Bellingham cops over their radio explain "He's coming --- He's coming – I don't think he is going to make it - I don't think he is going to make it" - Then there was silence over the radio.

I grabbed the mike of the State Troopers' police car to try and get more details of what they were witnessing. As we went by a couple of patrol cars parked along side the road, I recall seeing a couple of members come out of the ditch with their guns drawn as well. No sight of the stolen police car yet. I could see some broken pieces of wooden highway signs in the middle of the highway. Then I saw two sets of tracks going off the road to my left and through about 3 front lawns of residents in that area. The stolen police car had struck a house and was buried deep into the residence up to the windshield. An awful sight for me as I dreaded the thought of how I would have to explain all this to my superiors back in Canada.

The driver was unconscious in the car. The ambulance arrived and took the suspect out to hospital. I wanted to get the State Trooper I was with to authorize having the stolen police car towed out from the crash scene. He refused, advising me he had no authority to do this because this was on private property and he had no search warrant.

I turned to the Bellingham Police, who were in attendance as well, and asked them to authorize the removal of the police car. They also confirmed their hands were tied as they did not have a search warrant. At this same time, the owner of the damaged house came out the front entrance of his house in possession of a shotgun holding the barrel of the shotgun with his right hand as if to use it like a cane to support his stance.

He was either of Mexican descent or Spanish and demanded to get paid for the damages to his home. He did not want the car removed until he got paid. I knew I had a dilemma on my hands so I approached him in an attempt to gain his approval to remove the police car. I am sure he was fully aware I was a member of the RCMP because I sure looked a lot different than the local police he was used to seeing in his neighborhood.

I could not believe my ears in learning that the police had no jurisdiction to take the car out of this private property unless they had a search warrant. I asked the home owner if I could inspect the damage to his house and he allowed me into the kitchen. It was obviously a mess with the electric kitchen stove pushed into the middle of the kitchen showing electrical wires hanging out the back by a few feet. The corners of the room all had cracks from the impact and the kitchen floor was in ruin. It was a miracle no one was hurt inside the residence.

I asked the home owner what his estimation would be related to the amount of damage to his house. He hesitated for a moment and gave me a figure of about $2,000.00 dollars. My reply to him was that I felt the damages would more likely be in the neighborhood of about $3,000.00 dollars. He still seemed a little skeptical if he was going to be paid for the damages. I informed him that the Canadian Government has a lot of money and assured him that his damages would be paid for.

He seemed to agree and at that moment his level of anxiety dropped. It seemed like we had become friends when I told him I would make sure that the police car would get towed to a local garage in Bellingham and a seizure sticker would be placed on it. This seemed to satisfy the home owner who allowed me to authorize its removal from the impact location in the house. A tow truck was summoned to remove the police vehicle from the scene. By this time a lot of locals were gathering to see what had occurred.

In a loud voice I instructed the tow truck operator to have the police car towed to a local garage in downtown Bellingham and at the same time quietly instructed the tow truck driver to drive a block down the road, make a left turn and head back to Canada to have the car delivered to Cloverdale, B.C., which he did.

I immediately went to the hospital to check on my suspect, only to find he was still unconscious and being treated for minor injuries. I told the hospital staff to take blood samples from the suspect for blood alcohol analysis purposes in my investigation. Staff at the hospital refused to do this for me, sighting they had no authority to do this. I replied that I was a member of the Royal Canadian Mounted Police and instructed them to go ahead and obtain the blood samples. This was all the authority they seemed to need, and immediately complied with my request.

After returning back to my office in Canada I was devastated as to what events had occurred this evening. My thoughts turned toward whether I would still have a job with the RCMP in light of my junior service. There were at least 6 members in the office ready to help me put my statement together as to how events unfolded for me that evening. Each member would scrutinize my every word and offer a better way of putting my report forward. This was a major event and a nightmare in my career and I appreciated all the help I could get. My statement was given to my boss and all the paper work had to be submitted in light of writing off a police car. Theft of auto charges were prepared and the subject was processed for court.

The suspect pled 'Not Guilty' in court and chose to go 'Judge Alone' for a speedy trial process. When it came time for the trial, I gave my evidence in full detail. I knew I had a good case for conviction.

The accused used in his defense an argument that he was in the Canadian Army and stationed in Salarno Italy during the war. He was the commander of a tank and was hit by enemy fire causing him to receive a head injury. The tank had caught fire during this incident He was safely removed from the tank and taken to hospital where a metal plate was inserted into his head wound. He had survived this attack.

His evidence continued where he explained he could recall being in an accident and could recall being placed in a police car by a Mountie who told him to stay in the car where it was warm.

He explained the heater in the police car got hotter and hotter to the point where this triggered a memory of him being in the Tank back in Italy that had caught on fire. He thought he wanted to escape this environment so he decided to drive off with the car.

The Judge in his summation of evidence and overall examination of the case found the accused "Not Guilty" in this case.

The Force now took the position of suing this person for the damages to the police car. This litigation action resulted in the subject agreeing to pay for the damages by making $15.00 dollar a month payments until the total damage estimate for the police car was paid off. This resulted in the administrative file being held open for about 7 or 8 years until the books were finally closed on the case. My supervisor kept hounding me about the headache this file had caused him in keeping the file open for some individual to continue making $15.00 dollar monthly payments. Submitted by Regimental # 17496 - Retired S/Sgt. Paul Starek.

» » **Dogs eating dead man!** » »

I was working in Buffalo Narrows in 1988 and was training a new recruit. We got a panic call one wintery day from an excited female caller. She reported that somebody was dead on the road in front of her residence and that police should hurry as the dogs were eating this "dead guy". We headed to the reported location with red-lights and sirens and sure enough, hovered over a male lying on his back were 3 large mutts. As we approached we could see that the dogs were not eating the gentlemen but instead they were licking vast quantities of frozen mucus from the drunk's face. We took the individual into custody, gave him a bed for the night, and thawed him out. In the morning he got a meal and a cup of coffee. We suggested that in the future, when drinking, he should carry a handkerchief.

» » **Squirrel witness** » »

I knew a member who had a minor police car accident, hitting a stump alongside the road while on patrol. The damage was minor to the police car, yet an accident report still had to be submitted through various channels. For years, members sometimes laughed that some big black dog was running all over B.C., in front of police cars, causing them to lose control momentarily and consequently having an accident. That was not the case here; There were no witnesses. The member was instructed to put in a detailed sketch of how and where he hit a stump along the side of the road. In the sketch of the accident scene the member drew a stump along the side the road and draws a squirrel sitting on the stump. He remarks on the accident report that the squirrels were the only witnesses. The report went forward to Sub-Division Headquarters.

A week or so goes by and the member gets the report back with a request to go back and interview the squirrel sitting on the stump as a witness. I am sure this was just an exercise by H.Q. readers to poke fun at the member in the way he submitted his report.

» » **The Hats in there** » »

One member I knew was attending the office in civilian clothes when he was asked to assist us on a call of a drowning in the river. While assisting at the scene in searching for the victim, the member had lost his civilian hat. His hat had fallen in the water and sunk out of reach, just as he was trying to retrieve it from the water. He decided to put the cost of replacing his hat as an expense item on his next expense claim under this particular file. The cost was about $5.00.

The claim came back with a note that the hat was not an eligible item he could claim for. The member submitted the claim again, but this time with a lengthy explanation as to how he lost his hat while in civilian clothes and assisting on the drowning file. The claim was denied once more. The member became frustrated in the way the Force was dealing with this minor expense to him. He then took the step of submitting a normal expense claim at the end of the month that other members usually did. In his claim he included the usual patrol expenses such as lunches, dinners or midnight lunches while on patrol.

Upon submitting this expense claim at the end of the month the member lightly penciled in at the bottom of the report "The hat is in there somewhere - find it!" This was his way of letting the financial services branch readers know how ridiculous they were in refusing his earlier claim. He never heard back from them.

» » Goats milk for sale » »

In 1953, while stationed at McBride Detachment, there was anticipation that the Officer Commanding was to come and conduct an inspection of the Detachment. This was a yearly visit and the Detachment had to be looking its best. Unfortunately the garden located at the back of the Detachment complex was overgrown with weeds.

No attempts were made by the Detachment Commander to work the garden over or have someone come in to clean it up. This would cost money. One of the members stationed here was not all that fussy about doing physical labor cleaning up the weeds and came up with the suggestion that they should bring in a goat and tie him up in the garden so he could start cleaning up the weeds. The boss liked the idea as it would not cost him any money.

Arrangements were made and the goat was brought in and tied up in the garden. For some reason someone snuck into the back yard of the Detachment and untied the goat. The next day calls would come in that the goat was running at large somewhere in town and one of the members would have to go and retrieve it. At one point a call came into the office that the goat was found in an elderly lady's house standing in her bathtub. The goat was successfully recovered.

One day, shortly after this episode of events, the phone rang and I was asked if I had a good sense of observation. I told this subject that we were all trained to be very observant. This person stated he was puzzled over what he thought he saw hanging on the front door just under the RCMP sign. I went to look and found that someone had placed a homemade sign just under the blue and white RCMP sign. The sign read "Fresh Goat's milk for sale - Cheap".

The Detachment Commander came out to check this out and realized the goat situation was not in the best interest of the image of the Force. The goat had to go. In the end the Detachment Commander had to spend money out of his own pocket to get someone to come in and work the garden over just before the Inspector came for his visit.

» » "Joining the race" » »

It was during a local rodeo celebration in McBride, B.C. that I was asked to assist in getting the local horse race set to go. The ½ mile track was well groomed and several horses were getting ready for the big event. My instructions from the race coordinator was to start the race by shooting off my revolver. His instructions to the racers were "When you hear the shot, you're off.

I was on horseback near the group and could see the horses were excited. I discharged my revolver to start the race and my horse starts following the rest of the horses in the race. I was in uniform and tried to hold the horse back. We actually passed a few stragglers. After the race, I was told "If you would have won, it would have been a fixed race".

» » "The Sinking of the TOFINO" » »

The Force owned a patrol vessel named the "TOFINO" which was moored in storage at Ocean Falls, B.C. It had been moored for about three years while the Force was in the process of disposing of the vessel through public auction. I had visited Ocean Falls Detachment as a Section Head, which was part of the routine duties I conducted. Arrangements were made for a three man crew to come to Ocean Falls to pick up the vessel and sail her back to Prince Rupert.

As the crew was preparing the vessel for sailing with loading fuel etc, they noticed it was taking on water. The dry rot had taken its toll at the water line so as the loading of fuel caused the vessel to sink further into the water, more sea water was coming in. The crew scrambled to get the onboard pumps working but they were rusted and not functioning well. Additional scrambling took place to find nearby portable pumps to get the water out of the bilge area. I was at the Detachment office doing my routine inspection duties when the Detachment Commander came rushing in to advise me that if I wanted to see the "Tofino" one more time before she went down, I had better accompany him to the dock. He informed me she was sinking.

We rushed down to see the crew continue their attempt to save the vessel and in all the hustle, I saw one of the crew members busy; hosing down the deck of the vessel with fresh water. Someone hollered at him to drop what he was doing and help. Another crew member fired right back stating, "Don't bother him, if she goes down we want her to go down clean." The crew managed to save the vessel and make necessary emergency repairs so that the vessel could make a safe trip to Prince Rupert.

» » Man On the Bridge » »

It was in the winter of 1985/86 while I was a Corporal on a watch in Surrey. I was working a night shift with another member and after a busy evening we decided to take a meal break. It probably was around 1-2 a.m. We should have known better, but decided to go to Fresgo's restaurant on the King George Highway. As we stood in line to place our order your stereotypical 'Surrey type' came up and began asking if we knew anything about a fatal traffic accident a while back where his girlfriend had been killed. Evidently it occurred on the Delta side of 120th Street. I said that I hadn't heard of it, nor had the other member. The subject we were speaking to was drunk and became irate asking how we would not know of such a major event. I said that Surrey was a big, busy place and essentially would have no knowledge of an event unless I attended. He stormed off to sit with his buddy.

We got our food and began eating when this guy appeared at our table and began going on about our ignorance of events and our lack of interest. I pointed out to him in the local vernacular that he should take himself from our table or face a night in the slammer. Back he went to his booth, where he started yelling at us and then left. A moment later, he drove up in front of the restaurant window, honking his horn, giving us the finger and then he pulled out of sight.

We finished our meal and after leaving the restaurant, I said to the other member, 'Let's go up to the Dell Hotel, I bet we'll find that idiot there. Sure enough, there he was on a pay phone calling my S/Sgt to complain about me, I later learned. We drove past him in the marked police car and sat in the lot. He hopped in his car and drove off, and we nailed him for impaired.

Several years later I related this story to my 2 sons, one of whom is a New Westminster police member. Within 3 to 4 months of hearing this story, my son (NWPD) calls and says "guess who I just met today?'

My son had attended a call of a male who had climbed over the rail of the Patullo Bridge and was threatening to jump. He began talking to the guy and offered to get him any help he required if he would just get back onto the bridge deck. The fellow told him that he didn't trust the police after the way Surrey RCMP had mistreated him.

He then told my son the above story about the Surrey RCMP not recalling his girlfriend's fatal accident and that he had been picked up for impaired in 1986 and poorly treated. My son told him that the RCMP were like that, but he was a city policeman and would never be so dastardly. After some time, he managed to talk the guy into climbing back over the rail. My son queried the guy on the system and sure enough found the impaired conviction from Surrey in 1986 and that his father was the main investigator on the file, so it had to be the same guy. What are chances of something like that happening?

» » Horizontal Yellow stripe test » »

One member indicated he heard the local Fire Department usually holds in-service training sessions. On one training session it was learned the Fire Department instructor advised the class that they need to conduct the 'Yellow stripe' test before entering a scene. The learning objective here was: As you travel enroute to a scene, drive a little slower and let the police get there first. Then, as you approach, look to see if there are any yellow stripes that are 'horizontal'. If you see this, that means that the police member(s) have already fallen victim to dangers at the scene and you should approach with caution. If the yellow stripes are noted to be vertical, it is OK to enter the scene and conduct your duties.

After hearing this anecdote, I quickly recall a lot of members referring to the Fire Department or the Tow Truck Operators as the "Evidence Eradication Team". Now I can understand why some scenes are completely blocked off for hours until all the necessary data has been collected at a major motor vehicle accident.

» » Pull Over! » »

I was working Unit B highway patrol when it was located out of Burnaby. I was making a patrol in Langley. I pulled over to check a vehicle parked on the side of the road in an isolated area. The driver was asleep, sitting behind the wheel. I walked up to the driver's door and knocked on his window. He partially woke up and looked over at me. Seeing a cop startled him awake slightly more, and he remembered he was in his vehicle. He grabbed the steering wheel and started to rock it lightly side to side as if he was driving. I immediately started pretending that I was running on the spot - tapped on his window again - and started saying "pull over - pull over".

He did as he was told - he turned the wheel to the right - straightened - and tried to put the transmission in park (where it already was as the car was turned off.) I proceeded with a routine impaired, care and control case and charged the individual.

» » Elk Encounter » »

This happened to my recruit, (*yes they actually gave me one of those to train*). He is 20 years old, 6'4" and 155 lbs. I just came back from a 2 week course and this is what had happened to him as he described the event.

At about 10 p.m. one Thursday night, the town ambulance hit an elk 16 km north of town. They needed a member to go and put it down. So my recruit roared out there, using light and siren, to shoot his first elk. On the way there he clipped a different elk, scratching the left side of the Crown Victoria P.C. and the elk ran off.

He got to the scene, saw an elk thrashing in the middle of the highway. He pulled over to the shoulder. He reached down for his trusted 12 gauge Defender, it's not there, instead he found himself clutching onto a Snow brush in the gun rack. "Damn", he said.

He thought, "Oh well, let's go get this elk with my 9m.m." - mistake number 2. He drew his weapon got up to 3 feet from the elk and put 3 shots into the head area. The elk flopped down, "Good, she is dead."

He came around to her rear and reached for her leg to pull her off the hwy. She gave him a good elk kick, spraining his left thumb. He screamed in pain, swore a few times and went back to shoot the elk in the head area three more times.

So again he went around reached for the hind leg to pull. She kicked him in the shoulder so hard he flew backward landed on his ass on the middle of highway 40 with his pistol in hand. He swore again more profusely this time. The kick rendered his left arm useless. It went numb, he couldn't feel anything. Now he is angry.

In the meanwhile, the elk got up and started charging his way. My recruit got up and started running for the woods, turned back and shot at the elk 2 more times. The chase was on for at least 50 feet. Running and screaming, he got to the edge of the woods, dove in the snow and hid behind a tree and started shooting at the charging elk. He fired off at least 3 more shots. He could see the sparks coming off the asphalt. Not a good shot.

The elk came to a stop, so he took the opportunity to run back to the PC for cover. He climbed inside and shut the door. Then the elk came at him, head butting the driver window. We could hear the VIC camera audio "*&$ck, *&$ck - get away," and a whole bunch of gun shots.

He had rolled down the window fired off 3 shots from the driver seat. The head shot sprayed blood all over his hand and face. And now he is screaming because the gun shots perforated his ear drum. My recruit went to the hospital with a sprained left thumb, numbing of the left arm, scrapes and bruises, and perforated right ear drum.

He shot off a total of 14 rounds. The elk finally died of lead poisoning, and a couple of gunshot wounds between the eyes. My recruit learned very early in his career that when you get into that police car, you had better have all the tools with you to get the job done. From that day forward he made sure that the shotgun was in the police car before going on any future calls.

» » **Unforgettable Hit & Run file** » »

A 14 year old boy from Seattle was up visiting a cousin in the Chilliwack area. They were walking side by side along a fairly well used road in Rosedale at about 23:00 hours. They were walking with the flow of traffic when they were struck from behind. The vehicle did not stop and there were no witnesses. The boy from Seattle was killed instantly. The other was hit on his left side and had broken ribs and a broken arm. He survived but did not see anything and could not remember hearing anything. At the scene, we had no skid marks, no tracks on the pavement, no witnesses, nothing. I was working alone in the Agassiz detachment area and this occurred just on the border of our area and that of Chilliwack The Chilliwack guys came to assist. We all stood there trying to figure out how we could come up with something to help us get started.

Finally, one of the Chilliwack guys said there must have been something knocked off that vehicle. It was pitch dark, there weren't any street lights nearby so he started crawling on his hands and knees rolling his flashlight on the ground. We found a lot of dirt and pebbles, then all of a sudden he yelled that he had something.

We eventually found eight pieces of plastic. We thought they looked like they may be part of a car but we really had no idea. The largest piece was less than one inch long.

It was all we had so I seized it all, photographed the scene, even though there was nothing to take pictures of, and went home. I didn't sleep much that night. The next day I went back to the scene early in the morning to see if daylight offered any help. There was absolutely nothing - not a scratch on the ground. That day, I found out the deceased was an only child and he was a very bright young man. He had won a scholarship from NASA for science and was already planning his university studies long before he was due to finish high school.

His parents called me. The hospital contacted them requesting permission to harvest the boy's organs for transplant. The parents were crying on the phone and asked me what they should do.

I was not prepared for this, and almost fell apart on the phone. I managed to compose myself and bought some time so I could hang up and get some help from Royal Columbian Hospital (in the trauma center he was taken to). I was lucky that RCH has staff to deal with this and they offered to help me. They called the family back and dealt with it.

I went to see my Staff Sgt. I told him about the file and he could see I was upset. He asked me what I wanted to do. I told him I figured that only a person who lived in this area would use that road. It ran parallel to the trans Canada highway between Chilliwack and Agassiz so unless you lived nearby there was no reason to use it. Given the time of night the accident occurred, chances were the driver was local. I took the pieces of plastic to six body shops and eventually one stated they were 90% sure the pieces matched the grill of a GMC vehicle. They couldn't say whether it was a van or truck or what year it would have been. They gave me a 10 year spread.

I put an article in all the local papers and had other police officers in nearby detachments go out and speak to all body shops they could find. I wanted a call if anyone came in with front end damage that could be related to this incident.

Next, I told my boss I wanted to go door to door and I would speak to every human being living within a five mile circle. He asked how long that would take and I said I didn't care. He gave me permission to work on this and nothing else for one week, then we would evaluate our next move.

I started that afternoon going from door to door. If no one was home I marked the address on my map and came back later. I worked three 17 hour days, and was getting exhausted. Then I walked up to a farm house and knocked on the door. I had the piece down so it rolled out like I was a robot. AHello I am Cst. Dave Olson from the Agassiz RCMP. I am investigating a fatal hit and run accident where a young boy was struck and killed on Saturday night."

The man that answered the door just stood there. Then I saw tears running down his face. He started to cry but didn't say anything. It seemed like forever, but I guess it was only a few seconds. Anyway he started talking, going faster and faster. He said AI didn't know it was a person, I didn't mean to kill anyone@. I stopped him.

I caught my breath and asked him to sit down. We both sat on the floor of his porch. I read the standard police warning, arrested him and did all the procedural things I needed to do.

I was completely exhausted, I was emotional and I was in sort of a daze as I had given the same introduction to so many people and so far no one had any information at all. I just was not prepared to have him staring me in the face like that.

I had a tape recorder ready and he told me the story right there on the porch. While he talked I saw a GMC truck parked right in front of the barn, facing away from me. I wanted to go and look, but I had to finish. Soon I got what I needed. He pointed out the truck and said he was the only one with the keys and no one had driven it since the crash. I locked him in the back of my car and went to look at the truck. The windshield had a dent smashed into it, the size of someone's head. The plastic grill was broken near the headlight.

I knew I had him, but I had to secure the truck for evidence and get him to a phone to call a lawyer. I called for assistance and a Constable came to help. I didn't know how to deal with the truck but my partner said he would take care of it and all I had to do was get the prisoner back to the office. I took him in and gave him access to a phone to call a lawyer. He did, and then we talked. I gave him some water and he said he had not eaten in a long time. All I had was frozen TV dinners that we gave to the prisoners in cells. I put one in the microwave and let him eat it.

I was settling down but I was also elated. I had gone from what appeared to be a hopeless file to catching the suspect and all I wanted to do was go outside and yell for joy, but I had work to do.

I did the interview and he told me everything. He had been drinking at a local pub, and was so drunk he forgot to turn on his headlights. He didn't see the boys walking because it was so dark. Ironically he turned on his headlights as he drove away after hitting the boys. He said he could not believe he hit someone and he tried to tell himself it was a mailbox. He said that he saw the boy roll up onto his windshield in slow motion and then disappear. He said he was so drunk that he urinated in his bed that night.

Eventually the interview was done. I had the story but the accident occurred three days earlier so I couldn't do a breath test on this person. The only way I could prove he was drunk was from his statement. It was also the only way I could prove he was driving. I had him but it was a tenuous case. All it took was for his lawyer to come up with some reason his confession was not admissible as evidence and I was sunk.

The forensic exam of the truck was done the next day and I went to see it. We found the imprint of the seams and stitch marks from the victim's clothing on the hood of the truck. We found tiny amounts of blood and hair in the windshield, but the big one was the plastic pieces of grill. The eight pieces fit perfectly like a puzzle into the grill on the truck.

I called the parents, and I don=t know if it made them happier or sadder but I told them we caught the person responsible. I also warned them it would not be an easy case to win in court. I had to prove that he was the driver and that he was drunk at the time.

Later the family traveled up to see me at the office. They arrived a day early and I was not working that day but they called me at home and I came in to meet them. They wanted me to show them the scene where it happened, I was reluctant, but they insisted, so I took them out there.

It was awful for me, but they were stoic. I was close to tears when we got back to my office and the mother gave me a big strong hug. She thanked me for the work we had done and they left.

They all came back for court, and a woman from Mothers Against Drunk Drivers showed up with them. I was worried this would not go well, and they would be really upset. I gave my evidence. The forensic officer entered his evidence and we broke for lunch. I have no idea why, but after lunch the defense entered a plea of guilty.

I couldn't believe it. Anyway we got him for all counts, impaired and hit and run. He was sentenced to four years in jail and got a long driving prohibition.

The local pub always denied serving him any liquor and said he was sober when he left their premise. Obviously they were worried about being sued.

That was it. One I will always remember, because I worked very hard to solve it and never really expected to find him. I also didn't expect to win in court.

After listening to the tape recording of my interaction with the suspect in court the judge wrote a letter to my boss. He said he was impressed with my professionalism, he couldn't believe I was so good to this guy after being so wrapped up in a case like this. To be honest I have no idea how I kept it together. I got some good advice from my partner after he came out to help me, maybe that kept me on track. For a few minutes I actually felt sorry for the suspect while he was sitting there bawling but my sympathy didn't last. I just did what I had to do to make sure he went to jail. I got lucky in some respects but I also worked very hard to get this one done.

Maybe some day I will be able to forget about it, …….. that would be good.

PS: After receiving this story and going over the recollection of events, both the member giving me the story and I agreed, that it would not be hard to understand why some members, upon reflecting on their careers, would rather not go back to recount some of the horrendous experiences they went through.

» » Tale of a Dead Dog » »

Back in 1977, upon graduating from Depot, four of my troop mates and I were sent to Prince George Detachment. Shortly after completing our six month recruit field training, two of us ended up working on the same watch.

In June of 1978, in the early hours of the morning, I was dispatched to a call of a dead dog. The dog had been hit by a car on the highway, which was behind the owner's house, and was visible from the house.

Due to the late hour, the SPCA was not available to pick up the dog. The owner was concerned that her children would wake up in the morning and see their dog, so she requested that we attend and remove it. I attended the scene and found a rather large German shepherd lying on the side of the road, and it was in fact dead.

During our recruit training, I never did investigate a "sudden death" on my own, however, my troop mate had. As a prank, I called him on the radio and requested his assistance to investigate a "sudden death." He was more than willing to share his expertise with me and agreed to attend at my location. When he pulled up behind me on the highway, he asked where the sudden death was. I pointed to the side of the road and showed him the dead dog. At this point he realized that he had been made fun of.

He reluctantly agreed to help me pick up the dog and take it away. We looked through our car trunks for something to place the dog in. Not having any blankets, we decided to use a body bag. The dog was placed in the bag and put in my trunk. I then suggested to my troop mate that we take the dog to the garbage dump. He had different plans. He suggested that we throw the dog from the bridge into the Fraser river.

At 2a.m. we were parked at midspan on the bridge trying to get the dog out of my trunk. Though traffic was extremely light, a pickup truck did pull up alongside us and stopped to look. My troop mate told him to keep moving and get off the bridge, which he did. We watched the vehicle take the off ramp at the end of the bridge, which goes under the bridge and heads off in a different direction. As no other cars were coming, we took the bag out of the trunk, and on the count of three, heaved it over the side of the bridge railing where it fell a few hundred feet.

As we stood there chuckling, we heard the squeaking of car tires. It was from the pickup that we just told to get off the bridge. It had paused under the bridge and was watching us from below. I have never seen a vehicle take off so fast. This fellow just witnessed two police officers throw a body bag off a bridge.

We weren't laughing any longer. We were so scared that we jumped in our cars and took off. All I could think about was this person reporting the incident to our office, and we being such junior members, it would not go over well. I was pretty stressed for the rest of the night, however, I did think of a cover story. The plan was to tell the possible complainant, if he did come in, that we were setting up a "dummy bag" as a training scenario for our dive team. The team would be required to go into the river the next day and retrieve the bag. Fortunately, we never had to use this story and we never heard from that person. To this day, there is someone out there wondering what we threw off the bridge in a body bag. It makes for a great crime prevention initiative.

Well my troop mate, not wanting to be outdone by me, got back to the office ahead of me. He asked the front counter girl to tell me when I returned, that the owner of the dog wanted the collar back off the dog, for sentimental reasons. If I wasn't stressed enough, I was now. I told the front counter girl that the dog was in the dump and would be impossible to locate. I sweated for a couple of days before I found out I was set up.

My troop mate and I worked together for years both in Prince George and in Ottawa. We continued to play jokes on each other, I guess we never did learn our lesson.

» » **"I took one for the Team"** » »

My sergeant and I get called to a disturbance at a local nightclub, The Tudor Inn in South Surrey near the border. When we arrive, we come across two scantely dressed bimbos, who were drunker than a skunk, and ready for the drunk tank. They were having an issue with someone near the Club and were outside raising their voices. Upon arrival, I get there first and try to communicate with the first young lady while the Sergeant arrives and asks me "What do you want me to do?" I quickly instruct him to look after the other gal who just stepped around the corner of the Club and out of sight. I continue to gather what information I could glean from the first girl who was very vulgar with her language. I quickly get a handle on what the issue was.

As I begin to gain control of the situation, I see my sergeant come out from around the corner of the Club with this big grin on his face so I wander what had happened. He approaches me and says "I took one for the Team!". What he had encountered as he went around the corner was a full frontal view of a young lady who had her short dress up around her eyeballs and relieving herself in a squat position. She yells at the Sergeant "What the F**k do you want?" I thought to myself - Why do I always get the dirty jobs? The two girls eventually were placed in custody for the night as common drunks.

» » ATM Witness » »

It was about 1991/92 when I had a high profile bank robbery go down where two suspects entered the bank wearing ball hats, sunglasses, bandanas, scotch taped fingers and both armed with semi- automatic handguns. After vaulting the counter, they threatened to shoot the employees and customers and after obtaining about $3,000.00, fled the scene in a stolen vehicle.

I got to the scene and did the usual duties, including contacting Frisco Bay for copies of the surveillance tape. The Frisco Bay runner attended the scene and simply said he'd get me photos of the robbers committing the robbery dressed in their disguise, but that would be about it.

The next day, I received a call from a hysterical Frisco Bay employee requesting me to attend their office in Vancouver. Upon my arrival, the employee produced the photographs of the suspects dressed in their disguises committing the robbery, but further explained that they also developed the video from the ATM machine that was mounted just outside of the main entrance. Incredibly, it captures one of the suspects standing in front of the bank peeking inside without his disguise. He then walks over to the ATM machine and uses the reflective mirrored glass covering the camera as a mirror and slowly and methodically applies his disguise. He then obviously enters the bank and commits the robbery

I simply distributed the photo to other police agencies and corrections officials. It was the Matsqui Penitentiary who immediately identified the suspect as a known armed robbery suspect who had just been released from prison after serving a 10 year sentence.

We finally were able to get an address for him at a half-way house two days after the robbery and while on route to the half way house in New Westminster, the same bank gets robbed by the same two suspects. We set ourselves up at the half way house and got them returning home with the money, (bait money), gun and disguises.

When I interviewed the main suspect back at the detachment, he initially refused to admit to any robberies, but when I showed him the surveillance photos from the ATM machine, he sunk down in his chair and shook his head. I asked him what the hell he was thinking using the ATM machine as a mirror. He then asked me what an ATM machine was. After explaining it to him, he advised that he had just been released from prison after serving 10 years for bank robberies and they hadn't been invented the last time he was out! He didn't know what it was.

While awaiting trial, he took a female nurse hostage at the Surrey Pre-Trial Centre, where accused inmates are housed awaiting their trials. After a 5 hour stand off, the ERT team attacked his cell unit, where a stun grenade was lobbed next to him, at which point he instantly and literally shit his pants, then paid the price with a hard takedown! He received an additional 10 year prison sentence.

» » **Cover your tracks** » »

Some bank robbers just don't cover their tracks very well. Around 1990 an armed and disguised suspect enters a Guildford Bank and after pointing the loaded semi-automatic handgun at the head of a female teller, was given approximately $4,000.00 and fled the scene. This time an irate bank customer chased him out of the bank, but the robber stopped, turned and pointed the gun at the head of the customer, firing a single shot that missed this man's head by mere inches.

Needless to say the customer stopped his pursuit and the suspect entered a stolen vehicle and fled the scene. Units checking the area located the stolen vehicle abandoned in a cul-de-sac.

They conducted neighbourhood inquiries and were advised by a witness that the suspect exited the vehicle and ran down a walkway which lead to another cul-de-sac. The members canvassed that area and were advised by an elderly woman that she had observed a young woman sitting in a "blue vehicle" for the longest time, then this male ran to it from the walkway and they sped away. When asked if she managed to get a licence she advised she had not. As the members were walking away from her residence, the old lady advised the officers that it appeared that the female sitting in the vehicle was bored and while waiting for her male companion, was cleaning out the vehicle.

The witness then directed the officers to the location where the vehicle had been sitting where they discovered a neat little pile of papers on the side of the road. In the pile was an ATM machine printout for an account that was used 45 minutes before the robbery! We immediately contacted the bank's corporate security and obtained the details for the bank customer. He was checked on CPIC and came back to a well known bank robber living in Vancouver. We attended this residence with Vancouver City Police and arrested the male and his girlfriend, along with the bait money and the handgun. He was charged with armed robbery, possession of stolen property for the stolen getaway vehicle and attempted murder. Both received a 10 year prison sentence.

» »   **Work with what you got**   » »

In the Summer of 1985, I attended a single motor vehicle accident involving a motor-cycle just outside of Evensburg, Alberta. I had my mother along on a ride along at the time. I also had a prisoner on another matter in the back seat. Upon arriving at the scene I had to deal with a lady that had fallen off this guy's motorcycle. I took the opportunity to put my mother and the prisoner to work to put out traffic pylons and the prisoner was directing traffic allowing me time to attend to the scene. You work with what you got.

»» Arrest in Pyjamas ««

I'm aware of a member who was stationed at Stoney Plain, Alta and who was living in a small community, Onoway. A Break & Enter in progress call came in which was occurring in Onoway. This small town is about ½ hour drive from Stoney Plain so the Detachment phoned him to respond because he lived in town. He was in his pyjamas, as he put on his gum boots, attended the location with a shotgun and apprehended a suspect. It could be said he caught the suspect with his pants down as well.

»» Taxi! ««

Vancouver Airport - Immigration office incident. An Immigration officer was escorting two individuals that were detained for deportation back to India. These two subjects had made some sort of plan of escape. While escorting them through the airport terminal, one took off in one direction and the other in another direction. They had not been in handcuffs. The Immigration Officer caught one and told me to broadcast the BOLF (Be on the Lookout For) for the other suspect. One of our members was driving eastbound on the main thoroughfare heading away from the airport. Our member saw a subject fitting the suspect description in the middle of the median heading east on foot towards the city.

He stopped to approach the subject but surprisingly, the subject had jumped into the back seat thinking this vehicle was a taxi. This subject asked the driver to take him into town never realizing that he had jumped into a police car. Case closed.

» » John SMITH -Ya -right! » »

Mr. SMITH is such a common name amongst some individuals you deal with. In my career, every time I got involved with a "John SMITH", there was a twist to what was going on.

First when I was working security at the Vancouver Airport, before I was a member, a very drunk male came through. I felt he was too drunk to fly and called the RCMP. A member arrived, went down to the gate and arrested him for being drunk in a public place. No big deal right? I received a call the next day from the RCMP saying that the man, who was later identified as John Smith had died in their cells. This was my first witness statement I ever had to write for the police and it was the start of a string of John Smith situations.

The second John Smith was the body that I found in the Fraser River. In an attempt to determine who he was, my partner asked me to check his wrist watch as sometimes they may have their names inscribed on the back plate of their wrist watch. I checked and told my partner his last name must be "Stainless Steel". Our case file was named "Mr. John SMITH" until we could determine his true identity.

The third John Smith was a man walking on the highway in the middle of winter in Alberta miles away from anywhere. I was working Stony Plain Highway Patrol in uniform and driving a marked police car. When I checked him he told me his name was John Smith (right!) but could produce no identification.

He said he was American and told me he had just arrived in Canada and was just looking around. I took his information and released him while a NCIC and Immigration checks were done and kept an eye on him while I continued running radar (that really was the old days!)

When the NCIC came back they informed me the person I checked had been missing for over three years. When I drove up to him I rolled down my window and called out "John, come here" He ran at me and dove through the window. The fight was on.

I had my storm coat on and my seatbelt shoulder strap. I couldn't get to my gun because I was strapped in. The only thing I could do was roll up the window and trap him in the window. So there I was with my left hand holding the window handle tight and my right hand grasping for the radio. I grabbed the radio mike and called 10-33 (officer in trouble). Nobody responded. I thought to myself That's not good. I called 10-33 again and this time all the bells and whistles went off.

I guess the subject I was wrestling with heard the radio ruckus and let go, so I released the window handle and he slithered out and took off into the bushes. I called for a dog man and a subsequent search located him approaching a small village. He kept saying he was sorry he had attacked me but he didn't know I was a police officer. He was later diagnosed as mentally ill and was deported to the US hospital where his family was able to care for him.

»» Do manikins have ears? »»

I was a brand new member having just joined the Force. My parents had given me a gold watch as a graduation gift; the watch had my name inscribed on the back. I had not been exposed to dealing with a lot of sudden death calls at this point in my career. It was Sunday morning and a beautiful day. I was on a routine patrol near a river bank. Some guy was standing on the side of the road trying to get my attention. He had seen a body in the river. Upon first examination, I noticed that the head of this subject had no hair. This body at first looked like a manikin with clothes on. My question to the members back at the Detachment was "Do manikins have ears?." No one seemed to know, so we proceeded to remove the body from the water. The deceased was removed from the river and as we were trying to check for any identification on the body, I recalled that my parents had given me a gold watch with my name inscribed on the back of it. I turned to my co-worker at scene and asked him to check the back of the watch in the event he by chance had his initials or name inscribed on the back. My partner checked and replied. "You're right- It says "Stainless Steel". Talk about using black humour on the scene.

» » Trolling for Pigs! » »

In 1975, in a small town in southwestern B.C., I was working stationary radar on one of the two main streets with my partner. We observed a Ford convertible moving towards us at a high rate of speed, 52 miles per hour in a 30 mph zone. The pursuit was on and in a matter of a few blocks we had the vehicle pulled over. I quickly noticed there were four teenage females in the vehicle. I covered the rear passenger side as the cover member and my partner approached the driver and asked for the usual documents. I mentioned to my partner I had seen four unusual objects that were dragging from the rear bumper of the convertible.

My partner asked the driver what were these objects dragging from the rear bumper of the car. The drivers reply was: "They are corn cobs sir, we are out trolling for pigs and we just caught two!"

Needless to say, I had great difficulty, trying to contain my laughter but, my partner got so bent out of shape he not only wrote the female driver a Traffic Violation Report for speeding, but also a mechanical violation (Traffic Notice and Order), for a minor mechanical defect on the vehicle.

» » Letter of appreciation » »

This is the one that I will remember for as long as I live, and it is, and always will be the best reward of my career but I didn't find out until twenty years after the fact.

It was October 08, 1978, an overcast Saturday night in a small town in southwest B.C. I was working with only one other regular member on the shift as two others were off duty sick.. To make a long story short, my partner worked the North side and I worked the South side. I pulled a vehicle over and it turned out the female driver was drunk and a short time later she was charged with impaired driving. Sounds just like a normal shift doesn't it?

Twenty years later, October 13, 1998, when going on day shift at 07:00 hrs., I was going through my in-basket and found a letter addressed to Constable Reid. I opened the letter which contained a beautiful card and it read verbatim:

October 12, 1998

Dear Constable Reid,

This may seem odd, however I wanted to thank you for doing your job the night of October 8, 1978. You stopped me, and I was charged with impaired driving. I have been sober since that time, again thank you for saving my life and the life of somebody else, whose death I may have caused by drinking and driving.

Sincerely Lesley...

This letter is posted on my "wall of fame" in my house, as a great reminder to what I was taught as a boy, teen and an adult, and to others that may read it.

"Treat others the way that you wish to be treated", and "what goes around will eventually will come back around."

Cards like this are a great caption and reminder to any member's career.

I will never forget!

» »   **10 – 33 Code**   » »

She was just a fledgling recruit and her final physical test was to run the mile and a half within a certain timeframe to complete her program. To a lot of members this sometimes is seen as a threshold or a 'right of passage' of accepting them into the fold.

I was called out early that morning to a break & enter in progress. I didn't find the bad guy so I went back to the office at 0700 hrs and spoke briefly with the guard who told me that the boys arrested a bad one the night before and it took the entire night shift (2 guys) to get him into the cells. The guard said he was grouchy all night and that who ever lets him out in the morning would have a handful. I decided to go home first and freshen up etc. before I took on the prisoner.

I left and on my way home I see my recruit running towards the office. It was obvious that she was running her mile and a half test. I was proud of my recruit maintaining her fitness level. I continued towards home. Next thing I hear on the radio is a bunch of panting and wheezing "Ray - pant - pant – wheeze - 10....33".

I assumed that she had tried to let the prisoner out and that pandemonium had broken out and it must be serious. The guard was no slouch & I was sure he must be engaged in a life and death struggle with the prisoner. I turned around and returned to the Detachment, code 3, passing a semi-trailer unit on a blind corner.

I squealed into the Detachment office parking lot, red lights on. I bail out of the car and I see in the picture window of the office the guard sitting calmly in his chair with his feet on the desk. He sits up and notices me as I pull in. I burst into the office set to give him shit for not helping my recruit. He says" What's up?" I then see my recruit sitting over by the radio with her head between her legs panting and wheezing and she looks up and says "I just completed my mile and a half in 10..33" Meaning 10 minutes and 33 seconds. I asked her what 10.33 meant on the radio and she says "Oh Ya!... Sorry!" and then laughs. 10.33 is the common radio code for "Officer Down ".

» »   **I love you!**   » »

The life of a dispatcher carries many and varied experiences. This one memorable moment shows how some dispatchers might feel when contacting a member who is on call for duty.

It was a Sunday morning, 07:30 a.m., blue sky overhead and warm; the type of morning that invites you to breathe deeply and stretch. The Sunday morning peace was cracked by the alarms of the 911 lines ringing. There had been a head-on crash on the highway. Police and ambulance were sent immediately and confirmed someone was dead.

They needed the traffic analyst called from home and sent to conduct a thorough investigation. That meant I had to call someone out of their home.

This is a task dispatchers abhor, particularly in a circumstance such as this. When a regular member goes off duty, and on call in a small town detachment area. The officer expects to be disturbed. However, an investigator of this type isn't expecting a call, and what's worse is I know his morning is about to be split open by a very gruesome scene. Therefore, I choose to speak softly and sweetly when he answers the phone.

The officer is calm and professional throughout the call, taking all the pertinent details and asking for various resources which he will need. I can imagine my call to him has interrupted his Sunday morning sleep with his wife nearby. I continue to talk tenderly while we exchange all of the necessary information. I realize as we are hanging up that I may have overdone the 'soft touch' on the phone when he ends off by saying, "Goodbye, I love you."

I refuse to imagine what his wife must have thought!

» »   Telecom Center Abbreviations   » »

Telecommunication operators are a unique breed of individuals who are at the front line of policing. They carry the burden of disseminating information received, making quick decisions on the matter at hand and dispatching the information to the member on the road for response. Many of these support staff have been an integral part of the problem solving process making sure that the safety of the member on the road is paramount and also keeping a keen ear open to analyzing the type of call they receive.

Over the years I have had these pivotal staff give me examples of the short form abbreviations they have used in the Field depending on which environment they have worked in. Abbreviations have changed in some respects over the years but still are used by some telecom operators today.

ABBREVIATIONS USED IN FIELD BY OCC & MEMBERS

"K" Division - Alberta

CH - Concluded Here
NFAR - No Further Action Required
BOAD - Bit of a Dink
LNU - Last Name Unknown
C/N - Captionaly Noted

TITS - Too Intoxicated to Sign
BOLF - Be on the Lookout For
GOA - Gone on arrival
SUI - Still under Investigation
LPA - Left prior to arrival

"E" Divison – British Columbia

RCC - Report to Crown Counsel
OTSOP - Out There Somewhere On Pager
BOHICA - Bend Over Here It Comes Again
COM/SWAT - Complainant Satisfied with Action Taken
FBA - False By Attendance
CRAFT - Can't Remember a Fricken Thing.
SIL Mode - Screw It, I'm Leaving
CFL - Constable For Life
PIS - Prosecutors Information Sheet

OBS - Out Back Smoking
FIDO - F---k It Drive On
TTFN - Ta Ta For Now
DBS - Down Basement Smoking

RFN - Right Fricken Now.

ERT aka TFK - Trained Fricken Killers
FMA - Fricken Middle Aged
WGAFRA - Who Gives a Fat Rats Ass
A.H. - Agitated & Hostile (Ass Hole)
DHP - Dead Hockey Player (Tim Hortons)
TU - Tits Up - Radio is not working
TCO - Taken Care Of

FUBAR - F---ked Up Beyond All Recognition
MBWA - Management By Wandering Around
FABFA - Fricken A Bubba, Fricken A
MFWIC - Mother F--ker Who's In Charge
Oscar Foxtrot - Occurrence Free
ID10 T - Idiot!
NFG - No Fricken Good
10-7 No phone - Guys already dead
SCA - Stunned C—nt Act
FDM - Final Drip Mode (Coffee's on)
LPO - Loss Prevention Officer
DIPP - Drunk In Public Place

IGEFA - I Got Enough Friends Already
NFL - Not Fricken Likely
LTR - Little Tiny Radio
CYA - Cover Your Ass

DILLIGAS - Does It Look I Give a Shit
SG - Straight Goods
ISMH - I Shake My Head

UTL - Unable to Locate
10-100 - Pee Break
10-200 - #2 Break
ODS - Off Duty Sick
AOL - Absent On Leave

ODM - Off Duty Mad

CUNT - C. U. Next Time
TFS - Too Fricken Stupid

DWO - Driving While Old
Raisin - Old person
A & W - Alive and Well
LOL - Laughing out loud
Code Brown - Bathroom Break
10-15 - Mental Health Act
TH - Tim Horton's
7 Iron - Someone nowhere near a Driver!
SIIP - State of Intoxication in Public
JDLR - Just Doesn't Look Right!

TERMS USED BY THE PUBLIC ON HOW THEY DESCRIBED POLICE

MEN WITH NO LEGS: (Because they never get out of their police cars)

YOYO COPS: Because they go to the call and come right back to the office to do their reports as if attached to a string. One never sees them out and about talking to people.

WASPS / HORNETS: They see them leave in a hurry from their office and come right back just as quick.

SMOKIES: Used mostly in the USA.

CANARY LEGS: Probably because of the yellow stripe.

NARCS: Short form for Drug Squad members

PIGS: Common term used in today's society by the criminal element.

BULLS: Term that was used in the Prairies referring to police.

QUEENS COWBOYS: Probably still engrained from the March West.

»» Off Duty Mad »»

In recent years the RCMP has had to deal with members booking off duty sick for various reasons. Sometimes this would escalate to members going on stress leave to deal with whatever issue kept them from coming back to work. Recently, I have seen a change in terms surfacing while some members deal with various conflicts. The term "Off Duty Mad" has been mentioned as a condition where a member would simply quit working because they felt they had been wrongly dealt with by the Force. Managers and Human Resources had to closely monitor the steps taken to assess whether a member was fit to come back to work.

»» Mouth Wash »»

I had an impaired driving investigation and after having given the demand for a breath sample and putting the suspect in front of the breathalyser, the suspect took the opportunity to take a bar of soap from within the washroom and start chewing on it in hopes of getting rid of the smell of alcohol on his breath. Another member took control of my suspect and flushed out his mouth before I could conduct the test. People will do anything to try and beat the system.

»» Listen Up »»

My partner and I responded to a call of shots fired at moving vehicles. While en route I knew we didn't have things like Emergency Response Teams so we approached with caution. Upon approach to the area from either side I sighted the subject who matched the description. He was about 100 yards from a trailer which we believed to be his residence. He was not in possession of a rifle when I saw him. I decided since we had no communication with other members through portables, to rush the suspect. He began running for the trailer and he was faster than I had expected. I kept up to him but finally was able to trip him as he approached the trailer. Then the ground fighting started. I was ordering him to give up and all he was doing was groping on the ground. He appeared not to be cooperating with my instructions. I jumped on him the second time and began to try and choke him out. Throughout this I kept ordering him to stop fighting but to no avail. My partner arrived and we were able to subdue the suspect. He was reluctant to stand up and in broken English explained that he was looking for his hearing aid since he was legally deaf. So much for verbal judo, which is a tactic police officers use to communicate with suspects.

» » Fire in Cells! » »

There were only 6 or 7 of us on shift that night in Prince Rupert. It was a typical Saturday night with the usual calls coming in related to bar fights, domestics. It was nearly midnight when we get a call of a loud party getting out of control at an apartment block.

We had been at this address on previous calls weeks before so had an idea of what we were getting ourselves into. The manager of the apartment complex was frustrated on how to handle the rowdy group that were congregating at one apartment suite.

We attended the first time and gave fair warning that if things did not cool down we would have to shut down the party. The tenant agreed, however things did not go well after this. Within the hour of our first attendance, another call came in of the party getting out of control. It was time to act. We set up with as many members as we could, knowing we will probably have to arrest a number of them under Section 31 of the Code (Breach of Peace), or just Drunk in Public, (DIP's) we called them. The Guard was told to get ready for a busy night.

One of the members responding made contact with the manager of the apartment complex as we settled in front of the complex ready for battle. He agreed to cut the power to the actual suite where the party was taking place. What a beautiful site to hear the loud stereo die in such a fashion as if it had suffered a major heart attack or seizure. The lights went out and we could hear some scrambling and banging going on as we approached to try and disperse the crowd. Booze was everywhere and those with any sense of respect realized we were there to mean business so they quickly slithered off into the night to avoid arrest. We started picking people up for being drunk and loaded them into the paddy wagon.

My recollection is that we arrested up to 18 people on that call so a lot were destined for the Drunk Tank or placed in cells to cool off for the rest of the night.

With the Paddy Wagon and police cars full of drunks, we learned that a neighbouring tenant who was fed up with the loud party issue took advantage of the situation when the power went out. He had entered the suite to throw a few punches at some of the guests inside. This was about the same time police arrived to remove a number of bodies who were still not that willing to leave the scene.

Once back at the Detachment, the Jail Guard was ready for the onslaught of booking in prisoners. The book in sheets were ready for easy quick notes to be made of prisoner effects. I can remember all the pigeon hole portals being full, as well as a complete row of boots and shoes piled up in the hallway with a booking sheet and a bag with personal effects attached. It was a sight to behold with all the noise and commotion in the 'Book in' area.

I had gone back into the main office area to check on something with dispatch when I heard some yelling going on in the cell block area. "Fire!" was the word that rang out. I guess one of the prisoners may not have been searched well enough and started lighting some toilet paper in one of the cells to create more havoc in the cell block area. "Fire!" was the call from within the cell once again. One of the senior constables saw this as an opportunity to grab the fire hose from the wall near the 'Book in' area and commenced to spray water at about 5 or 6 cells, where a number of prisoners were standing and yelling. By the time I got back towards the cell block area, the constable yelled out loud, "Is it out yet?", and nailed the contingent of prisoners one more time with a blast of water, making sure they were all soaked to the point of looking like wet chickens standing in a rain shower. It was a cool night at best and the humidity within the cell block area had that musty stinky smell of wet socks.

What a beautiful setting for the prisoners to settle down for the night. The yelling and insults continued for better than an hour as they all realized they will have to put up with being wet and cold as the morning hours wore down for their eventual release when sober.

As the daylight hours approached, all subjects were released when sober with a few still sighting they were treated poorly for spending the night in the slammer. We stayed professional as possible stating that the "Crow Bar" Hotel had only certain amenities that were available in light of the circumstances. Another successful midnight shift had come to an end without major incident for the Detachment Commander to look into.

» »   **Time to Pay is Up!"**   » »

I had an individual who was given a fine for an offence that was serious yet not that serious for him to spend time in jail. He was given 'Time to Pay" by the Magistrate however he was "In default", which meant the deadline for the fine to be paid had come and past. I tried to locate this subject but could never find him at home.

I went to his employer and asked if he was prepared to pay off his fine and take it out of his future wages. The employer asked if he could pay the fine 'One day at a time' as his employee was not that reliable. I told him that this was not a suitable arrangement so the employer replied "Well I guess it's up to you to find him then!"

I would check for my suspect at all hours of the day. I went to his place where he was known to periodically hang out. People claimed he was not there. We left the residence and returned within a matter of minutes but this time parked the police car a little further away and approached the house quietly. I went to the front door and my partner took the back door. The front door was unlocked and I slowly went into the house. I heard noises coming from the master bedroom. We both entered the room and I saw a set of feet disappear through a trap door into the attic. I yelled out "Who are you?" and the subjects reply was "I guess I'm the guy you're looking for." Subject was taken into custody to deal with a few days in jail in lieu of paying his fine. Case closed.

» » X-Rays identified the Victim » »

Boston Bar, B.C. 1971. I was stationed at a two man Detachment in the interior of B.C. when I received a complaint from a father who was reporting his son as having left home and he had not heard from him in a while. The father believed his son was in the area, and stated that he was the type of individual that would ride the rails and would frequent this area. The father had received some mail from him postmarked Boston Bar as a return address. I went to the postmaster who confirmed an individual had been picking up some mail but could not give me an address. If you ever wanted to know anything, or pick up on the local gossip, the local postmaster had a handle on things. I was told that frequently a lot of individuals that ride the rails lived in a "Hobo Camp", located about two miles out of town and alongside the river near the tracks.

There was no other way to check local sources to confirm if this subject was in the area. I checked the hobo camp but could not check the specific area as at this time of year. There was about 4 or 5 feet of snow in that area. I told the father we would check things out in the Spring as that particular area was uninhabited during the winter months.

The next Spring I managed to reach the location I now believed to be the area of the "Hobo Camp" where this fellow had supposedly lived. I contacted a few 'locals', who were first sceptical of my appearance on the scene but eventually I learned from one 'hobo' exactly where a certain cabin burnt down last Fall. I discovered the old make shift cabin that had burned down. When poking about a bit I found what I believed were the remains of an upper torso or chest cavity of a fire victim in the burned out ruins. I didn't know for sure if this was the person that had been reported missing earlier in the Fall, but this was all that remained of whomever had lived there.

Our records indicated the missing person had been in a Federal penitentiary. Any person who is convicted of a criminal offence and is sentenced to a federal term, more than 2 years in jail, must have a chest x-ray. Armed with this information I had the local authorities take an x-ray of the chest cavity remains I had recovered. In discussing the matter with the coroner the local radiologist compared the x-ray from our known subject with the remains found in the burned out cabin.

We were able to positively identify our missing person as the victim in the burned out cabin. The radiologist was able to make the positive identification from an old back injury suffered by the victim years earlier. I then visited the father and gave him the sad news.

» » Aggravated Assault » »

I had to investigate an assault involving a couple of teenagers. The father of the suspect kid was upset at me for charging his son, so he called my Cpl at the time. My Cpl and I met the father to listen to his concerns. The Cpl explained what happened in regards to his son being arrested. The father then says," Well, I still don't understand why my son was arrested. Isn't this aggravated assault?" The Cpl asks," What do you mean sir?"

The father goes on to say," Well, my son was aggravated by the other boy so he assaulted him." My Cpl and I look at each other and wondered "Is this guy for real?"...

» » Still driving in a snow bank » »

I was on patrol and driving in a blinding snow storm near Selkirk, Manitoba in the mid 1980's. The snow coming towards the windshield would almost hypnotize you. I had a new member with me who wanted to see the ropes of doing highway patrol duties.

Up ahead I spotted a car in the ditch, with lights on and one lone male occupant. After approaching the car in about 3 feet of snow, I noticed the driver, who showed obvious sings of impairment, in a trance and probably believed he was still driving in the snow storm. The motor was running and the rear tires were spinning in the snowbank.

I decided to have some fun with this one and decided to approach the driver's side of the vehicle. With my flashlight wrapping on the window, I opened up the driver's door and told my suspect to "pull over'. The look on his face of bewilderment was something to remember. As he looked over and saw me standing in the snow with my yellow striped pants, I'm sure he was in astonishment that I could run so fast to come up beside the car.

He immediately put on the brakes and began to move the steering wheel to the right as if to pull over and stop. He placed the vehicle in park. I went through my usual routine to conduct an impaired driving investigation while in care and control of a motor vehicle.

The accused in this case hired himself a high-profile lawyer out of Winnipeg. On the day of the trial, the lawyer showed up while a large contingent of locals sitting in the courtroom were waiting for the show to start. Unfortunately, as soon as this lawyer read the details of the case just before the trial started, he stood up and entered a 'guilty plea' on behalf of his client. Too bad, I would have liked to have given evidence on this one.

» » "Why didn't you call the Police? » »

My partner & I were on patrol in the downtown East side of Vancouver in the Summer of 2000. We responded to an arson call. Upon arrival at a low rental hotel, we discovered the ambulance had already taken a subject to hospital from the small room in the hotel where a fire had started. The hotel was a mess, 2 night clubs on the bottom floor had water damage on a Friday night.

In order to get some sort of idea on what had really occurred my partner and I went to the hospital to interview the victim of the fire. He was a mess with both arms bandaged at the wrist.

My conversation went something like this.

> "What happened?"
> Victim: "I was depressed"
> "How long have you been depressed"
> Victim: "About 13 years".
> "We need to know what really happened up there?"

> Victim: "Well, my life was not really going all that well this week, so I tried to kill myself by cutting my wrists. I couldn't find any veins on both arms, so I gave that up and tried hanging myself off the water pipes and the pipes broke when I jumped off the bed. Then, out of frustration, I figured I would light the mattress on fire and maybe die of smoke inhalation."

"You have gone to a lot of trouble to try and do yourself in; You cut your wrists, you have scar marks around your neck from trying to hang yourself Why didn't you just call the police?"

Victim: "I thought I had to do something to get the attention of the police so I tried doing those things."

"You know that all you had to do was call the police and ask for help"

Victim: "I didn't know I could do that!"

We both looked at each other and thought, "Some people never cease to amaze you".

» » **What Goes Around – Comes Around** » »

After retiring from the RCMP I was working the front counter as a Complaint Taker & Information Officer at Surrey Detachment. A person came in to report for the first time as a parolee. When I asked what his background and history was he replied that he had done time for possession of stolen property. After processing his documents he wanted to know what had to be done to report a break and enter. He had been staying at a local half-way house when his roommate, and now a suspect, was suspected of ripping him off. He had his television, stereo, etc stolen. The first thing that came to my mind was 'If you fly with the crows, you get shot, or 'if you sleep with the dogs, you catch fleas'. What really caught my eye was that this victim had actually picked up a pamphlet entitled "dealing with breaking and entering - a pamphlet for victims". …Priceless!

» » **Moose Left Bad Omen** » »

In northern Manitoba, members went on patrol to check out a story of a moose that was found frozen into the ice at the edge of a lake. They discovered the animal had somehow become stuck in the mud and had died where it stood. Winter set in so the animal remained frozen in this state. Local First Nations who trapped in the area felt this was a bad omen

After her B+E, Ruth was glad she'd invested in a good lock. Cuz without it, they would have taken everything!

Murray Macauly
Kamloops RCMP 1193

CHAPTER #16

Embarrassing Moments

»» Neighbourhood Watch Meetings »»

"Neighbourhood Watch" was a buzz word in the mid 1970's where Detachments started up Crime Prevention Unit programs to keep the public happy because they were becoming victims of crime more often.

I was running a Neighbourhood Watch meeting in Kamloops one evening and had an older man, about 72 years old show up late. He only lived about a ½ block away from the school in a trailer park. You could tell he was out of breath when he came in. It was a short meeting because on this occasion the old fellow who came late wasn't even settled in his seat when he lay his head on his neighbour's shoulder and quietly went to sleep. I knew something was wrong so I stopped the 16 mm film projector I had just started and went to the aid of this man but it was too late. Moments later he died from a massive heart attack.

The guys back at the office came out with the usual black humour and were giving me a hard time with comments like "I guess the old timer was either bored to death or was dying to see you!!"

»» False Alarm Robbery »»

In an effort to gain more knowledge on how to run a Robbery Seminar I took the opportunity to go to a neighbouring Burnaby Detachment and watch a couple of Crime Prevention members put one on. All the bells and whistles were in place. There appeared to be an enthusiastic crowd ready to take part. At the beginning of the lecture all seemed to go well until the back door to this 3rd floor hotel lecture room swung upon and into the room wandered a man dressed in jeans, jacket, unshaven and carrying a 45 calibre handgun. He approached the guest speaker, took his tie and fled the room. All this was done to create a teaching point of how much people really remember when they are asked to describe someone. Moments later I could hear sirens of all kinds near the hotel and then the fellow setting up the little scenario went scrambling. What happened after this little demonstration robbery was not communicated to various authorities including the dispatch at Burnaby Detachment. One of the janitorial staff saw this man leave our lecture hall carrying a 45 cal handgun and reported same to management. Police were called and everybody and their dog was converging towards the hotel. The constable setting up the scenario had to do some fast explaining to dispatchers back at his own police office to cancel the call as unfounded. Crime Prevention Officers since than have taken other steps to prevent undo concern when setting up such training scenarios.

» »   They're gaining on me!   » »

A Native Special Constable is on patrol in the Creston Detachment area. He was referred to sometimes by the locals as an "Apple", because he was red on the outside and white on the inside because he worked with the Mounted Police. On occasion he would head out to the Reserve to conduct some sort of enquiry before the rest of the shift started. He reports to dispatch "Creston from 16, I've got a high speed chase on the go here - can you send some help?"

The members at the detachment were getting themselves organized. They could hear his plea for help while getting ready in the locker room. Moments later a second call came over the radio "Creston from 16, is that help coming because they're gaining on me?" - Someone was chasing him off the reserve!

» » Bear Facts » »

At Chilliwack Detachment in the 1970's - members lure a bear cub into the back of a prisoner van and drive back to the detachment parking the van in the detachment garage where you would normally park to unload prisoners. They go into the detachment and set up the rookie on shift to go and remove the drunk from the van and place him in cells. The members did not plan on the rookie leaving the inside door open to the detachment from the garage so when the back door of the van was opened, out came the bear and headed right into the detachment office. A typewriter was almost destroyed by the bear looking for an escape as well as the front plate glass window to the detachment. The NCO was called and advised of what happened. His reply was "As long as the typewriter is replaced and the window repaired by morning I'm not even aware of what happened". Hours later all was repaired and the dayshift continued on as normal. I feel sorry for the poor guys on the shift that had to foot the bill for repairs.

» » Beeper Message » »

Two Burnaby members responding to a sudden death near the bridge find a suicide victim. He had taken his life with a firearm and to say the least was missing most of the top of his head. The victim was laying underneath a flat bed tractor trailer unit in an industrial area. What made this situation so unique to members attending was that fact that as they were waiting for the coroner's vehicle to arrive, the victim's beeper went off a couple of times. When the Coroner arrived and initial examination was complete, they checked the beeper and discovered the message was from a female with a high pitched voice that said - "If you got any more brain cells left in your head you'd be home for supper by now." How do you write this one up in your sudden death report?

»» Doggone complaints »»

A Member in Surrey responding to a call of a suspicious nature where the operator noted that there was a call coming in with heavy breathing on the other end and some immediate dog barking. The member attended the residence and found the home locked and two dogs going nuts inside. As he was deciding what to do the owner pulled up and wandered what was wrong. It was later deducted that the dogs had somehow pushed the phone off the table causing the receiver to come off the phone. After a short while the operator cut in and asked if anyone needed assistance. To this the animals came up to the receiver and were heard breathing over the phone. They began barking as soon as the voice on the phone asked further questions. Chalk this one up for responding to barking dog complaints.

»» What are you looking at? »»

A Drill Instructor at Depot Division who had done service in Surrey Detachment was aware of a young man who was being transferred to Surrey for his first posting. He had seen his father, who was a retired member give his son his badge on graduation day.

Just before the young constable left Depot for Surrey, the Drill Instructor approached the young man and forewarned him that when he gets to Surrey Detachment, he will meet a Training NCO who has very large ears.

Instructions were left for him to ensure that when he first meets this Corporal, he should not make any attempts to focus on looking at his ears because this Corporal is very sensitive about this if he notices one looking at his ears. The constable took this advice under his confidence and proceeded West.

The Drill Instructor than gave me a quick call at Surrey Detachment and explained to me what he had just done with the young Constable. He had witnessed the young man's father give his son his badge on graduation day and both embraced each other in front of the crowd. The Drill

Instructor wanted me to ensure that at the very moment he comes into my office, I should immediately challenge him on what he was looking at, intimidate the young man and at the same time go and give him a big hug thereby welcoming him to Surrey Detachment. It went like clock work. The young constable came up the stairs with anticipation that he was about to enter my office. I have to admit I do have large ears and took this opportunity to embellish my displeasure at the instance he laid eyes on me.

"What the hell are you looking at Constable? I then got up to approach the young man who at this point looked like he was a little in shock. I reached out and gave him a hug and welcomed him to Surrey Detachment. I than proceeded to explain how he had been sucked in to a set of circumstances, compliments of his old Drill Instructor.

» » Who let the dog out? » »

In early 1970 I was stationed at Vancouver Drug Section when a telex from Ottawa arrived. The Telex advised that a D/Commissioner had decided to have labs trained as drug detector dogs and Vancouver was to get one. The NCO I/C was to identify a drug member to handle the dog. Being a dog lover I volunteered and soon found myself off to the training kennels in Alberta. Upon arrival I was introduced to a frisky black lab by the name of BART, PSD 66 and I was advised that BART had already been trained and now it was my turn. In three weeks we were a team and headed back to Vancouver.

BART lived in the back yard in a Force supplied kennel and was the pet of the family. Several months later I left on a course for 2 weeks with the care of this highly trained PSD in the hands of my wife. When the course finished I called my wife and when I asked how she had made out with the dog it became evident that something had happened. After ensuring her I would not get mad or upset she advised me that one day, as per custom, BART was let out of his kennel to get some exercise in the yard. The fence is not too high, so you had to stay in the yard with him as he liked to wander. The phone rang and in she went, only later to return to an empty yard.

She was terrified. She had lost a highly trained PSD. Into the family car and after much searching, there, on the side of the road was what she was searching for. She got out and called the dog and it came right over and jumped into the car.

Relieved, she drove home and locked the dog in the kennel to deter any more problems. About 2 hours later she went into the back yard and when returning to the house she checked to make sure the dog was still safe and sound. She noticed that something was not just quite right. The dog looked different! Upon further and closer examination, it was not BART and in fact was not even the right gender. She had kidnapped someone else's dog, and a female at that. She quickly bundled the dog into the car and drove to the spot of the kidnapping and as inconspicuous as possible released the dog hoping she would find her way home. She drove around the block and there was PSD 66 BART, playing with some kids in a local school yard. He was returned to the kennel and I don't think he got too much exercise until I returned home from the course.

» » Are you Dead – or something? » »

In Burnaby members responded to a sudden death call. They found a deceased person in his residence who had been dead for some time. The subject was quite ripe and the smell of death was heavy. As members tried to piece together the subject's last movements and to determine time of death, one member happened to examine the deceased's telephone answering service and out of several messages this one message really stuck out. "Where the hell have you been old buddy, are you dead or something"?. Investigating members got a kick out of this.

» »   Oops – Wrong Building   » »

An early morning raid on a drug flat in a Northampton, U.K. High rise. The eight officers, equipped to break down a flat door on the ninth floor had taken the 'Bosher', a large metal device made specifically to put through doors. They had started the climb into the elevator to the target floor. Other officers were already located on that floor and positioned to cover off the stairwells and approach from the sides awaited for the 'strike' command with eager anticipation.

The elevator clicked over the floors and the number 9 appeared in the frame and the doors opened to the radio command 'Go, Go, Go'..... The eight officers launched noisily into a hallway totally unoccupied and enjoying utter silence at this 6 a.m. early hour until that point.

The radio burst into life.... Where are you? We don't see you? Have you got the wrong floor?.... No we are on target and ready here on the ninth floor of Claremont House...... The silence that followed was then punctuated by a response.... Err.. Perhaps if you could make your way to Beaumont House (the adjoining high rise) we could start over!!!

» »   Weird name!   » »

After getting transferred to Nelson B.C. I remember doing one of my first traffic stops and asked for the driver's name. The driver gave his last name as "BETHCHIKOCKOFF". I was not ready for this and thought to myself - Is this for real?

» »   Rightful pay   » »

On a certain reserve the Chief took it upon himself to hire someone from the village to keep the loose dog population down and agreed to pay $1.00 for each dog that was shot. Reportedly the person who took on this task apparently shot some 50 dogs in one day. At the end of the day the Chief asked the individual why he didn't pick up the dead animals after shooting same. This individual replied, "For another $1.00 a piece I'll pick them up and take them away."

»» Preventing further abuse »»

It was the beginning of October when I was called to a report of an assault. The 73 year old female victim wanted to meet me at a Tim Hortons Doughnuts location. I met her to gain more details and gathered as much information as possible. It was the usual situation, the victim in this case complaining that her husband had been pushing her around and in fact stood on her toe. She proceeded to show me her bandaged toe. A lengthy discussion followed covering the nature of the incident and whether there was enough to deal with for future charges. There was discussion about the possibility of a peace bond. I stated that this may not be appropriate as they were still living together and that the court order primarily would prevent both of them from direct contact with each other. After hearing this the victim exclaimed. "Oh don't worry Cst., My husband and I haven't had direct contact with each other since Christmas.

»» Not too swift »»

The young constable was observed walking back and forth in front of this small business location. He was pacing in such a fashion as to give notice to others nearby that he was giving deep thought as to what might have happened. The incident was one of a report of break and enter and the complainant was standing by waiting for Identification members to attend. The business had a garage door and a small window that was cracked open for ventilation. It was secure and there was no sign of forced entry. As a backup officer arrived the complainant approached this member and asked him why the other member was pacing back and forth.

As they approached this investigating member he remarked, "I just can't figure it out, I just can't figure out how the culprits got that battery and tools through that small crack in the window." The backup officer was so surprised at hearing this that he quickly removed this member from the scene to avoid further embarrassment. It was obvious that culprits removed the stolen goods by simply lifting the garage door and left the scene. Some days one can't see the trees for the forest.

» »   Bear Patrols   » »

At Revelstoke Detachment regular patrols had to be make patrols to the local dump to keep the general public away from getting the bear population upset. On one occasion the patrol car pulled up and the two members got out to send people away as they were at the dump watching the bears. This was working OK until one member got a little too close to send a young bear cub on his way as well. It started running away for a short distance however I guess the bear cub stopped in its tracks and asked itself, What the heck am I running for? The cub turned around and started towards the members. Both members hightailed it back to the police transport however in this instance they crawled in the back seat of the police car, closing the doors behind them. The front door to the police car was still open so guess what, the bear cub took it upon himself to become patrol Sgt. and really tied into the front seat. The members were protected alright in the prisoner compartment of the rear of the police car but help couldn't be summoned. Minor damage to the front seat of the car including the radio system etc was all the bear could accomplish as he left his mark and departed. Surrounding witnesses leaving the dump area had something to talk about after this patrol.

» »   Seeking forgiveness   » »

Over the years I have heard a number of members provide a quote "You can get forgiveness quicker in this Outfit than you can get permission!". It was their way of dealing with situations as best they could to ensure the job got done, never mind the policy.

» » Encountering a slick intruder » »

In the fall of 1992 and I from Surrey Detachment were dispatched to a break and enter of a residence. When we arrived at this south Surrey residence we were greeted by two very concerned elderly ladies. We asked them to stay at the front door while we secured their home.

On a quick inspection we found a few small planters on the window sill had been knocked over and other knickknacks on the bookshelf had been knocked over. On the kitchen table was a wicker basket with an apple and a pear in it. Both were half eaten. We checked the remainder of the living area and found all doors and windows secure. We toured the bedroom and found nothing had been disturbed there.

We entered the living room to interview the two ladies when I caught movement out of the corner of my eye in the kitchen. The kitchen curtains were moving as I approached them and I quickly pulled them back. I had found our suspect... It was a squirrel!!

The squirrel jumped onto the kitchen table and then onto the floor. I scrambled after it on all fours, finally getting hold of it to only be bitten by the squirrel. I let go and the chase was on. My partner was frantically kicking at it as it darted past him and into the bedroom. We were right behind it and quickly shut the door. Mission accomplished!, Yeah right!... The lady looked at us and said "I can't sleep in my room with a squirrel in there!". Both of us looked at each other and shrugged, It would only take a minute. Yeah right!...

We went back into the bedroom and shut the door. I removed my jacket so that I could use it to trap him with. The place was "hide and seek" heaven. It had a bed, couch, dresser, two night tables and a mattress propped against the wall. My partner would make a noise or move something in order to scare the rodent my way. The first attempt was a failure. I was on all fours when he darted from under the bed, gave a couple of head fakes, leaped over my jacket, crawled down my back and dove into the closet. I quickly shut the closet door.

Our next plan was to kneel side by side and block the closet door when we opened it. Another failure, It came out in a blur, went between us and back under the bed. Now it was all out warfare. We began banking furniture and yelling and scrambling around on all fours trying to capture this thing. It ran back and forth as we fell and rolled. I laughed so hard I was near tears. I don't know what the two ladies were thinking with all the clatter that was going on.

Finally I said to my partner, "Let's either call the SPCA or shoot it". Then I noticed another door in the corner and it opened to the outside. We propped it open and stood back and waited. A few minutes later out came the squirrel, panting and wheezing, he made it to the doorstep. With a wary look over his shoulder he turned and was gone into the night. This was one file we didn't have to report on.

» » **Head On Collision!** » »

A member in "K" Division was travelling southbound on #2 Highway from Edmonton towards Calgary a few years ago. His speed was the same as that of a southbound train so he thought nothing of it. As the miles past he could see the trains speed was as constant as the patrol car's speed. The member became very alarmed when he spotted another train coming from the South and heading northbound. He immediately got on the radio and with a sense of urgency broadcasted to the dispatch that they had better get a hold of the ambulance, fire trucks and other resources as there was going to be a hell of a big train accident that he was about to witness. Moments past as the member watched both trains coming at each other, neither showing any signs of slowing down. The member anxiously watched and than reported that he had made an error in judgement. He did not realize that there was a double track.

» » A Police Officer Speaks » »

An article printed in a newspaper in the USA by a State Trooper serves as a salute to the millions of police officers who put their lives on the line for us everyday.

> Well, Mr. Citizen, it seems you've figured me out. I fit neatly into the category where you've placed me. I'm stereotyped, standardized, characterized, classified, grouped, and always typical.
>
> Unfortunately, the reverse is true. I can never figure you out. From birth, you teach your children that I'm the bogeyman, then you're shocked when they identify with my traditional enemy... the criminal! You accuse me of coddling criminals... until I catch your kids doing wrong.
>
> You may take an hour for lunch and several coffee breaks each day, but point me out as a loafer for having one cup. You pride yourself on your manners, but think nothing of disrupting my meals with your troubles.
>
> You raise Cain with the guy who cuts you off in traffic, but let me catch you doing the same thing and I'm picking on you. You know all the traffic laws... but you've never gotten a single ticket you deserve.

You shout "foul" if you observe me driving fast to a call, but raise the roof if I take more than ten seconds to respond to your complaint. You call it part of my job if someone strikes me, but call it police brutality if I strike back. You wouldn't think of

telling your dentist how to pull a tooth or your doctor how to take out an appendix, yet you are always willing to give me pointers on the law. You talk to me in a manner that would get you a bloody nose from anyone else, but expect me to take it without batting an eye.

You yell that something's got to be done to fight crime, but you can't be bothered to get involved. You have no use for me at all, but of course it's OK if I change a flat for your wife, deliver your child in the back of the patrol car, or perhaps save your son's life with mouth to mouth breathing, or work many hours overtime looking for your lost daughter.

So, Mr. Citizen, you can stand there on your soapbox and rant and rave about the way I do my work, calling me every name in the book, but never stop to think that your property, family, or maybe even your life depends on me or one of my buddies.

Yes, Mr. Citizen, it's me... the cop!

The author of this article was Trooper Mitchell Brown of the Virginia State Police. He was killed in the line of duty two months after writing the article.

»» Are you Ms. ***'s Lover? »»

My neighbour happened to be an elementary school teacher, single and good looking. She was brave enough to ask me to come to her school one day and deliver a short talk to the elementary school group during police week. After getting settled into the classroom and fielding a few questions, one youngster from within the group had his hand up and I allowed him to fire away with his question. He hesitated a little and then asked with a concerned look on his face. "Are you Ms. ***** lover?" I was perplexed by this young boys concern and only replied that I was a good friend of hers. You have to be ready for anything when you go to a school talk.

»» Surviving a Street Sweeper »»

A well-known Vancouver police officer with a huge reputation for being a character is reported as being on patrol one night with his Harley Davidson motorcycle. These bikes are a fairly large bike with all the bells and whistles attached. The storey is told that one night this officer pulled up alongside a carload of individuals that caught his attention. He had just passed a street sweeper that was busy cleaning the parking area of the street. As the member waited for the traffic lights to turn he was surprised to learn that the operator of the Street sweeper had not noticed the motorcycle in front of him. His focus perhaps was more towards the curb. As the sweeper began making contact with the back of the bike, the member had no time to jump off and quickly decided to place the bike on its side allowing the street sweeper to continue forward and go completely over the member and the bike. Needless to say, he was the topic of much discussion over the years for having lived through this ordeal.

» » Feedback on training course » »

After retiring from the Force I had the opportunity to set myself up as a Training Consultant and for a number of years delivered Field Coaching Courses to various policing agencies across the country but mostly in Western Canada. In 1996 after finishing a 3.5 day course, one of the candidates on the course presented me with a document in which he expressed his vision of what he had learned. While his comments carried a message to me to clean up my act in terms of the way I expressed myself during the course as a facilitator, I got a chuckle out of the full meaning of his thoughts.

I realized he had incorporated in his comments the exact comments I sometimes made during the delivery of various topics taught throughout the course. The comments referred to are in italics.

"Rogy- We'd like to thank you for coming to pass on your experiences. Before we had this course, training a Rookie *has sometimes been as frustrating as batting fog*. Now some methods of how to train a Rookie have *hit us like a sheet of plywood*. Although *there are all sorts of pin holes in the pipe*, we know we can do some *spot welding* to fix them. We know that if things go wrong, we can always go back to *'ground Zero'*.

Those days when we get a Rookie who could not *drive his finger into a lard pail* or who *sits there with a far away look like a dog peeing over the cliff*, we know *it will all shake out in the wash*. We also know that *no one can be absolutely useless, they can always be used as a horrible example*.

There are lots of *umbrellas you can hang your hat on* and hopefully most of the information we have picked up *will stick with us like shit to a blanket*.

Remember – *training a Rookie is like NIKE management, "Just Do It"*, otherwise *you will be up to your ass in alligators with one oar in the water!!!"*

» » Oops – Sorry! » »

A few years ago I worked with a member in Surrey who wanted to help an individual out. A individual was spotted sitting on the front lawn in a residential area. The member approached this male who was obviously inebriated to the point that he would have been placed in cells if seen in public in the downtown area.

The male was approached and asked what he was doing on the front lawn to which he quickly replied that he had locked himself out of his house and could not get back in. This drunk indicated he had left his keys somewhere. It turned out that this drunk used to live at this residence he was sitting in front of. The member promptly kicked the front door in and allowed the drunk to enter the residence. The member left thinking he had done his good deed for the night.

Moments later an elderly lady called police in a frantic stated advising that someone had just kicked in her front door of her house and there was now a drunk who was collapsed and sleeping on her couch. Members quickly responded and that is when it was determined that the first member who helped the drunk out realized he should not have kicked this door in to let the drunk into the residence in the first place. The drunk was removed and taken to cells as a result. This situation would have cost the public purse a few dollars as the member had to put in a report for damage done to this lady's door in the line of duty.

CHAPTER #17

You Had To Be There

Police Officers who reflect back on their experiences take great pains to give detail on how an event occurred only to add that the significance of the experience was one where "You had to be there to appreciate what went down!" For this reason the following stories are included.

» »   **Backwards S/Sergeant**   » »

The S/Sgt of the small northern detachment lived about 7 kilometers out of town. He was experiencing problems with his small Datsun Pickup. It seemed that the standard transmission would get stuck in one gear. One morning while he was on his way to work he had put his vehicle into reverse to back out of his driveway. The gears wouldn't shift into forward after that. He ended up driving backwards into the town to report for work. Talk about dedication.

» »   **Crazy Glued Gun**   » »

A female member who was a Firearms Instructor in Ottawa worked with a lot of VIP Security members during a routine firearms training session. She challenged one member to check his firearm on a regular basis. This was important as the Force had just switched over to using the new 9 MM pistols instead of the .38 calibre Smith & Wesson revolvers. The member remarked he never checks his weapon as he never really has a need to pull it out of his holster. In this instant, she had the member demonstrate that he could in fact check his firearm to ensure it loads the chamber. He reluctantly drew his firearm in the process of showing her he could do this and found that the gun was jammed. He tried again and finally gave the firearm to the instructor to see if she could open up the chamber. It could not be done. The firearm was sent to the Armourer to have it repaired. The armourer discovered upon examining this members firearm that it had been totally glued shut with crazy glue. An investigation followed as to who could have done such a thing. It certainly had the member concerned as to the seriousness of the incident. What was learned was that the member was having marital problems. Although it was never proven, it was highly suspected that the member's ex-wife may have been responsible for using crazy glue to glue his firearm shut.

» »   Pony Tail restraint   » »

A member stationed in Coquitlam, BC about 1986 recalls one of his coworkers had arrested a combative type and handcuffed the subject from behind. In the back seat of the police car on the drive to the office the guy starts to attempt to kick out the rear side window. The member stops the police car, opens the door on the side where the prisoners head is and thinks about overpowering him again but realizes that the guy has a long pony tail. He calculates out how tall the guy is, reaches in, grabs the pony tail, pulls it out the door so it is just outside, then slams the door on the hair, holding the bad guy in position so that he cannot reach the other side window with his feet. Problem solved.

» »   Shots Fired Call   » »

We both responded to a "Shots Fired" call near the Putello Bridge in Surrey, B.C. It is late in the evening and the city lights cast some light in the general area of the industrial land adjacent to the bridge. This area of town has a history of unusual incidents where serious offences have taken place. After checking the area we thought we spotted two individuals near the beach and on the other side of the bush near the bridge. We felt these individuals might have a possible weapon in light of the call we were responding to. We approached the two and took them down at gun point. After cuffing both subjects this is what we learned. They both had been fishing on the Fraser River that evening and needed to go ashore to relieve themselves. It just so happened they were entering into the Surrey policing jurisdiction. As they were standing there relieving themselves they noticed a police car approach and within minutes were taken down at gunpoint. The one subject, while being handcuffed, had his face sideways in the sand and remarked to his buddy "How do you like Surrey so far?" - Priceless. Both were released after looking at the situation and realizing the two individuals had nothing to do with the call we were responding to.

» » **Police Harassment Enquiry** » »

Recently, RCMP King's Detachment in Nova Scotia, ran an e-mail forum (a question and answer exchange) with the topic being, "Community Policing."

One of the civilian email participants posed the following question, ***"I would like to know how it is possible for police officers to continually harass people and get away with it."***

From the "other side" (the law enforcement side), - the late - <u>**Cst Sandy Horsnell, obviously a cop with a sense of humor, replied:**</u>

"First of all, let me tell you this... it's not easy. In the Annapolis Valley, we average one cop for every 600 people. Only about 60% of those cops are on general duty (or what you might refer to as "patrol") where we do most of our harassing.

The rest are in non-harassing departments that do not allow them contact with the day-to-day innocents. And, at any given moment, only one-fifth of the 60% patrollers are on duty and available for harassing people while the rest are off duty. So roughly, one cop is responsible for harassing about 5,000 residents. When you toss in the commercial business, and tourist locations that attract people from other areas, sometimes you have a situation where a single cop is responsible for harassing 10,000 or more people a day.

Now, your average ten-hour shift runs 36,000 seconds long. This gives a cop one second to harass a person, and then only three-fourths of a second to eat a donut and then find a new person to harass. This is not an easy task. To be honest, most cops are not up to this challenge day in and day out. It is just too tiring. What we do is utilize some tools to help us narrow down those people which we can realistically harass.

The tools available to us are as follows:

PHONE:

People will call us up and point out things that cause us to focus on a person for special harassment. "My neighbor is beating his wife" is a code phrase used often. This means we'll come out and give somebody some special harassment.

Another popular one is, "There's a guy breaking into a house." The harassment team is then put into action.

CARS:

We have special cops assigned to harass people who drive. They like to harass the drivers of fast cars, cars with no insurance or no driver's license and the like. It's lots of fun when you pick them out of traffic for nothing more obvious than running a red light. Sometimes, you get to really heap the harassment on when you find they have drugs in the car, they are drunk, or have an outstanding warrant on file.

RUNNERS:

Some people take off running just at the sight of a police officer.

Nothing is quite as satisfying as running after them like a beagle on the scent of a bunny. When you catch them you can harass them for hours.

STATUTES:

When we don't have PHONES or CARS and have nothing better to do, there are actually books that give us ideas for reasons to harass folks. They are called "Statutes"; Criminal Codes, Motor Vehicle Codes, etc… They all spell out all sorts of things for which you can really mess with people.

After you read the statute, you can just drive around for a while until you find someone violating one of these listed offenses and harass them.

Just last week I saw a guy trying to steal a car. Well, there's this book we have that says that's not allowed. That meant I got permission to harass this guy. It is a really cool system that we have set up, and it works pretty well.

We seem to have a never-ending supply of folks to harass. And we get away with it. Why? Because for the good citizens who pay the tab, we try to keep the streets safe for them, and they pay us to "harass" some people.

Next time you are in my town, give me the old "single finger wave."

That's another one of those codes. It means, "You can't harass me."
It's one of our favorites. (Posted in honor of the late constable HORSNELL)

» » Wake Up Call » »

In Regina, Saskatchewan, my trainer and I respond to a call of a sudden death at a private care home that looked after the elderly. It is the middle of winter so when we get into the front lobby of the residence we see a stretcher set up with a body on it and a white sheet over it. In the corner is a neat pile of personal clothing and personal effects that no doubt belong to the subject we were called in for. My partner and I take some initial details of who the individual was. Being the good trainer that he was he wanted to make sure all was in order before we called the coroner to get permission to remove the body. He moves the white sheet back from the body and places his two fingers alongside the neck to check for a pulse. I guess his hand was cold from handling the police car door in the cold frigid weather. This act caused the old man to wake up. Both of us jumped back in shock realizing that the elderly gentleman was mis-diagnosed by home care staff. The cold fingers were enough to awaken the old man from his deep sleep. I will never forget that moment.

» » Squeeze Play » »

This happened at North Vancouver cells. This girl was in the female cell being held for some investigation. Each cell has a lunch box door which is a hole in the door just big enough to put a lunch box or toilet paper through. Rounds are made every fifteen minutes to check on everybody. In that time frame the female prisoner managed to fit half her body through this small unlocked opening. When she was found she had to get pushed back in as she was stuck. She was bruised and scraped from her head to her waist. When asked where she thought she was going, she replied "I was bored and wanted to see if I could fit ".

》》   **Water tastes crappy**   》》

Two members stationed in Saskatchewan respond to a call and while enroute hit a moose. Both members are seriously injured with one member remaining in hospital in a coma for a couple of days. His family and friends are at his bedside in the hospital visiting when the member wakes up from his coma. One of the family quickly gives him a sip of water. The patient takes a drink and smacks his lips as if to suggest the water does not taste very good. He takes another sip and gives the same reaction. He finally takes out his top dentures and discovers that moose dung residue was still lodged in the top of the dentures.

》》   **A true hero**   》》

One of my duties since retirement has been to conduct security interviews for those who are applicants for security clearance so they might have access to a police office. In this case I was interviewing a 50 year old who was a contractor. He appeared for this interview in his working uniform. His background check reflected nothing out of the ordinary. There were a few entries listed under his name but nothing adverse surfaced to cause me concern.

As I got into conducting the security interview I learned this man was a bit of a loner who lived by himself and minded his own business. He was well respected by his peers and past employers. There was some evidence of him being a 'week-end worrier', meaning that he enjoyed his beers. It was also learned that a number of years ago he was a heavy drinker and now seemed to have managed his drinking pattern responsibly.

As this person drew a picture of how he has lived his life, it quickly became apparent that he had experienced a lot of things in his life especially during those teen age years living in Winnipeg. His parents died years ago and he had no contact or knowledge of any other siblings or relatives other than some distant uncles. At an early age he witnessed his parents continually fighting. When asked to describe the biggest crises he had ever faced in his life, he replied that when he was about 7 years old, he had to break up a fight between his mother and father after witnessing her trying to stab him during their argument. It was shortly after this that he was placed into a group home for young boys as he was made a ward of the government through the Children's Aid Society.

He went on to describe that growing up in this environment led him to get involved with the law. His most difficult years were from the ages of 14-17 years. He was into experimenting with different types of drugs and doing breaking and entering as a young offender. He recalled being placed on probation by the Judge and given a suspended sentence.

He took a moment to advise me that during those days, (about 1970), when he was in trouble with the law, he met a Winnipeg City police officer who interacted with him on a regular basis on the street. The Cop knew about his past and tried to steer him in the right direction seemingly aware that there was potential for this young boy to make sound decisions and stay out of trouble. He stated that every city has a cop like that and he was lucky enough to meet such a cop. He recalled this cop took a liking to him and stated that when he was checked on the street one day, he took out a personal calling card he had, gave it to him and stated that if he ever had any notion of getting into trouble or doing something stupid, he should find one of his friends and make arrangements to come to the cop's house so that he could play pool in his basement. The cop told him that he had told his wife to give him permission to go and play pool in the basement if he showed up at the house.

He was impressed by this gesture of good will and trust and remembered that he had full intensions of going there to take advantage of this offer. Within two weeks of receiving this card from this cop, he had learned that the same cop was stabbed to death while attending a domestic disturbance. He was shaken by this outcome of events and took the time to go to the court case to see what had taken place.

He recalled during the trial and sentencing of the accused, that the cop's wife and widow, stood up and asked the courts to be lenient on the accused because that is what the cop would have wanted. This turn of events left a strong impression on this man's mind for many years. He concluded this storey by saying that every city has a cop like that and he considered the one he had encountered to be a true hero.

» » **Inside the Musical Ride** » »

Picture this:: The Musical Ride has had many characters who create history within this mystical group which is a symbol of pride for the nation. They sacrifice their time away from home to entertain audiences across the world. The workload sometimes is hard as the horses need constant attention. Everything has to look neat for the next show.

Generally every year about 30% of the Musical Ride members are replaced to bring in a fresh contingent for a 3 year commitment to the Ride. It goes without saying that this group of members slowly become a tight knit family who work as a team. Every once in a while a newcomer arrives and leaves the impression that they do not really have to pull their weight in doing the chores around the stable. This is where the fun starts.

Most family members will police themselves in terms of challenging each other to pull up their socks and 'get with the program' so to speak. It just so happened this one member did not get the message which caused a bit of a rif amongst some of the team members.

A few took it upon themselves to teach this person a lesson by 'shit troughing' or 'horse troughing' the person. This is commonly known as some sort of 'hazing' practice to teach someone that they had better clean up their act or they will pay the price through peer group pressure. The horse trough is simply a large metal container that contains water for a horses to drink from.

It came to a head one day when some of the members grabbed their target team member who was not producing that well even though he/she was not heeding verbal warning from others to buck up. The 'shit troughing' took place which is not a pleasant experience to say the least. One's uniform becomes soiled and wet and the whole experience is a humiliating one which hopefully taught a lesson. This one exercise caused a minor scuffle between two members at the time it went down where one member received a punch in the face during the exchange of comments at the time of the incident.

The group involved would disburse and go about their business hoping the target member had learned their lesson and realized they had better pull up their socks and get back into the fold of being a team player. One member of the group decided to have some fun with this from a group moral perspective so he arranged to have someone dress up as a roving reporter wearing a trench coat, a fedora, including using a microphone of some sort. He had someone video tape this character interviewing several horses in their stalls to get their reactions to what they saw during the 'shit troughing' incident that occurred earlier.

Picture a video clip with voice over conversation between a reporter and a horse where questions were asked of the horse in the following manner. The horses head was in a bridle which was nudged downward to make it look like the horse nodded in agreement to comments made. At the same time another member would place his hands about the horse's lower lips making it look like the horse was actually talking.

This exchange of conversation between the horse and the reporter was well edited to ensure those who watched the video had a hilarious laugh while they reflected back on their earlier experience. The video clip sounded something like this:

Reporter: Any thoughts or comments on what you just saw happen this afternoon?

Horse: You should have seen it! It was a thing of beauty to watch!. I even seen a couple of punches thrown at what's his name!

Reporter: Do you agree with the treatment that was handed out?

Horse: Sure thing. anybody that does not pull their weight around here in cleaning up the horse shit deserves to get 'shit troughed'. It's the only thing to ensure everybody chips in to get the job done as a team.

Reporter: How do you think your other neighbouring horses feel about what they just saw?

Horse: I noticed a few of them chuckling under their lips thinking the same thing I was. It gets boring standing around here waiting for the next show. We like a little action now and then!"

» »   **A 'Routine' Traffic Stop?**   » »

Many times you hear about the routine traffic stop. As we all know, they never are, and this one was no exception.

We were just off the hooker stroll in the Strathcona area of East Vancouver. Ahead of us is an old Caddy driving slowly and a bit erratically. After following for a while, my partner and I decide this car needs to be checked, something is not right.

We hit the lights and wait…. Nothing. A couple blasts of the phaser from the P.C…. Nothing. A yelp of the siren. Finally the car pulls over. Due to the delay, my partner says to watch myself with this one. He will deal with the driver; he wants me to watch the passenger as we can see two people in the front when we hit the takedown lights.

Approaching with care, I listen to my partner for any signs of concern. He starts to talk to the driver, and I can hear his voice change. His attitude is not one of concern, but I can't quite figure it out. The car is an older one, with a weak suspension and is riding close to the road. You can't see the faces of the people unless you go out of your way to bend down and look in the car. This makes the situation even stranger.

My partner pops his head up with a huge grin on his face. Obviously not a sign of trouble I deduce. He asks me to have the passenger step out and get their information. A bit strange as our responsibilities are usually contact and cover, and let the regular member deal with the suspects.

I lean down and knock on the window. A second later it slowly rolls down. I ask the person to step out of the vehicle. The person hesitates, making me wonder what is going on. I ask again saying that they must step out now, looking for compliance, my heart starts to beat a bit faster, waiting for the unknown.

The door pops open and I help it open all the way. I look down to see pumps, the ugliest legs ever, and a worn, wrinkled dress. Not very attractive at all. The passenger turns to get out and I now understand my partner's grin. The passenger is an elderly man well into his sixties in full drag! Lipstick, eye shadow, earrings, the works. It seems he and the driver were out on a 'date' when we came upon them.

He was speechless as he exited the vehicle with my assistance, pleading with his eyes, and finally his words to let him stay in the car. I guess he was a bit embarrassed with all the attention they were getting and just wanted to go home.

The driver, also in his late sixties was checked for sobriety, warned about his driving manner, and they were released to continue on wherever they may be going.

» »   Duty in Las Vegas   » »

I was excited about my new status as a reserve police officer with the Vancouver Police and was curious to see what was out on the internet in the way of resources that I could use to improve on my own knowledge.

Being a big computer user and having access to the internet I came across a list-server that was private for police only. This included reserves and retired members, so I send the required ID to the host and was given access to the list. This is basically a large email system that everyone on the list gets copies of any mail sent on the system.

About a year later, I found out I was going to Las Vegas for a contest I won from work. I would be spending 5 days in Vegas with a number of others from the company and would have a bit of money to spend while there.

Not being a gambler, I was trying to figure out how I was going to kill all this time in a city like Vegas. Then I had an idea. I went to the list-server and sent a message out stating I was going to be in Vegas for a while and if was there anyone from the local department that might be interested in setting up a ride for me if they do such a thing. I got an immediate response from a Sergeant who was more than willing to show me around and get me hooked up with a shift.

I got ready for the trip, I packed my personal body armour, handcuffs, search gloves, and flashlight wanting to be as prepared as I could for the big city. I just hoped my bags wouldn't be searched at the airport and have to explain all of it. The badge and ID would be going too, just in case.

My contact arrived at the hotel with his young son in tow. We had lunch and talked about the city and how it differed from Vancouver. I found there really wasn't much of a difference between the two cities other than the fact that the casinos were a focal point in Vegas. They experienced the same types of calls I saw in Vancouver, however how they dealt with them were different due to the types of resources available to them.

My contact delivered me to the North Las Vegas Metro office. This office included in its patrol area the Vegas strip with all the casinos. I thought this would make it very interesting seeing the action behind the scenes at the casinos as we undoubtedly would be getting calls there.

I was brought into the roll call and introduced to the shift as a member of the RCMP! I quickly correct them and helped them understand that the Mounties were not the only force in Canada. It is true that the further south you go, the less our American friends know about Canada.

I was assigned a host for the shift and after a quick trip to the locker room to don my body armour, we headed for the patrol car. After a quick check of the equipment, my host for the evening approaches with a backpack. He opens the bag and says "which one would you like"? I am not sure what he means until I look in the back and see an assortment of handguns. He says if I am riding with him, he wants to make sure I can help if we get into trouble!

I look at him as if to say are you sure and he advises that he has already told the team I would be carrying so they are aware of it. It seems they are a lot more relaxed with gun control for police in the States. Everyone that I spoke to on the Vegas team carry at all times, even when off duty. It's something that is a given once you are sworn in.

In addition, although they make a suggestion as to what you can carry while on duty, they are given an allowance towards the purchase, they can basically carry whatever they want to use.

That said, he hands me a small .32 caliber handgun with a concealed carry holster for my vest. While I am busy installing this under my armour, he walks to the front door and pulls out the department issue shotgun. He turns to me and says "This is yours too, it's in the seat rack between us, loaded and ready to go, I will use this".

My host opens the rear door of the patrol car and unzips a long case. From the case he pulls out a completely tricked up shotgun. Night light, sling, custom stock. He turns to me with a big smile and says that this is his bad boy. I think I just landed in Neverland.

Everything ready to go, we head out on patrol. The night continues on with calls very much like Vancouver. Domestic, motor vehicle accidents, break & enters and assaults. The one outstanding thing missing is calls to casinos on the strip. It seems that casino security is given a lot of power and there are few times the police actually have to deal with problems. I wouldn't believe it if I hadn't seen it, or the lack of it.

The night was nearing an end when the radio suddenly goes nuts with calls about a drive by shooting. We are close and start heading that way when another unit advises they have the victims stopped at a nearby intersection. We arrive and I see my first gunshot victim with a few holes in the car plus one in a leg.

My host starts to ask questions of the driver when he suddenly takes off for the car calling for me to hurry back with him. When I get in, he tells me that another car is behind the suspect vehicle at a nearby intersection and we are going to assist in a felony stop!

My heart starts racing as we head to the intersection only two blocks away. We will be the second car and the lead unit is only one man. He wants my help on the stop so grab the shotgun. I grab the shotgun from the seat rack and pump a round into the chamber. The adrenaline is flowing now as we roll up on the intersection.

The suspect vehicle is to the left of us with the other police car behind it. They are waiting for a green light. We slow and stop at the intersection and when the light turns green the suspect vehicle starts a left hand turn. Emergency lights are activated on both police cars and the suspect vehicle immediately stops. We jump out of the cars and I take a position up behind the car covering the passenger side of the vehicle. Then it hits me.

I am a Canadian citizen in plain clothes with a shotgun aimed at people that have just shot at and hit at least one other person. The chances of this going really bad are good and I am in the thick of it. Try explaining this to a judge I am thinking.

My partner for the night calls the driver out of the car. He complies. He is cuffed and put in the other car. The passenger is then called out. He is struggling and I see that he has an artificial leg and can't move as quickly as he is being asked. I let my host/partner know this and we slow it down. The passenger is complying so the stress is decreasing, but there are still 2 or 3 people in the car.

It feels like half an hour has passed, but it has only been a couple of minutes since we stopped the car. I look to my right as I have heard a couple of cars stop and want to see what is happening. The sight is like a scene from a movie. There are SWAT members all over the place. Full SWAT gear, balaclavas, M16s, and dogs.

I decide now is a good time to remove myself from the situation and quietly move back into the shadows and let the SWAT guys take over my position of cover. I am still nervous as now I am with a bunch of cops that don't know me, I am in plain clothes, No ID showing, and I'm carrying around a shotgun. Not the best place to be at the moment!

They clear the car, make the arrests, all without incident. Not a bad way to end a night.

» »   **Behind the scenes – Shelving attached**   » »

The Officer Commanding "D" Division, Winnipeg Manitoba, made a submission to the associate editor of the Quarterly where he related correspondence between two senior N.C.O's over material that was needed to build shelving. Here is the copy of the memo in its entirety dated May 16th, 1957.

Re: R.C.M.Police Quarterly

Recently, one of the N.C.O's stationed in Divisional Headquarters supplied me with a copy of an amusing exchange of correspondence between a senior N.C.O. i/c of a Northern Detachment and the Quarter Master of "D" Division. It seems this matter arose at the time Divisional estimates were being submitted, and Churchill Detachment had to specifically report upon the board feet of lumber which would be needed to construct shelves. Obviously, some confusion arose over the terminology used in connecting with this item. Quoted verbatim are the letters which these N.C.O's exchanged.

> "Many years have sped by since I joined the Force
> And I'm rapidly reaching the stage
> After grooming a horse and a CPC Course
> That recruits even think I'm a sage.
> But the jargon abuse the Supply Office use
> That horrible example (it's one for the books)
> I mean 'Lumber for Shelving attached'.
> Our Patrol NCO has five stars on his arm
> And now one regards him as dull.
> Why, he even knows what's in R.R. & O's.
> He quotes from the Code just like Knull.
> But he made it quite that he had no idea,
> As his balding old noggin he scratched.
> No, he hadn't a clue just like me and you
> What was 'Lumber for Shelving attached'.

The end of July is approaching on wings,
Our estimates soon must be met.
The pipeline debate will just have to wait
If our diary date isn't met.
I can even foresee how much it will be
To have the Detachment re-thatched.
But tho' blood I've perspired
I don't know what's required
For: 'Lumber for Shelving Attached'.

REPLY

The estimates were due as everyone knew
By the first of July for sure,
But lo and behold to our surprise we're told
To some the requirements weren't clear.
Now we must admit without losing face
That Patrol N.C.O's have their place,
And appropriate the fact that you used tact
When appealing to this learned place.

Now 'Lumber for Shelving' would seem quite clear
But the word 'attached' makes it confusing,
And we gather from a memo received this date,
That the problem is not amusing.

The matter has been discussed by the staff in stores
All of whom were agreeably surprised,
To find that our N.C.O.'s in the field
Admitted defeat, though disguised.

In dealing with Shelving you must bear in mind
Altho' some can be moved there is no other kind,
And that is the kind that is causing you grief,
So now I will try to take care of your beef:

When shelving's attached it is nailed to the wall,
And that shouldn't puzzle a smart man at all.

1. Since this is an actual incident which arose while dealing with an official problem, it is felt that the Editor of the Quarterly might wish to consider it for publication in the Section of the Quarterly "It Happened in the Force"

Signed: ******* Insp.,
Associate Edit "D" Division

The Commissioner,
R.C.M.Police, Ottawa, Ontario.

Attention: The Editor, R.C.M.Police Quarterly

FORWARDED, 16-5-57, for your information and that of the Editor of the Quarterly as suggested in paragraph 2 above.

Signed ******** A/Comm'r
Commanding "D" Division

» » I Gotta Puke! » »

While on Highway Patrol in Manitoba I picked up a suspect and proceeded to take him back to the office for a breathalyser test: I usually turned the interior lights down on dim so the suspect would not see how fast I was driving: After a short while the suspect spoke up from behind the 'silent patrolman screen' and made the following statement: "Stop this jet – I gotta Puke!"

» » Lone Ranger Call Sign » »

Fish Cops (Department of Fisheries & Oceans) certainly take their job seriously. A few years back, in the Summer of 2000, my partner and I were responsible for boarding vessels on the south coast of Newfoundland to inspect vessels suspected of repeatedly exceeding their catch limit of cod. This at least was the case in the last 7 landings. I went aboard this vessel to conduct my inspection of the fisher's logbook. Sure enough, another violation was obvious so I pointed the infraction out to the fisher. I immediately cautioned and extended rights to counsel to the skipper. The skipper seemed very agitated and confused by the investigation. After the catch had been off loaded approximately $10,000.00 worth of Cod, Skate & Monk fish were seized.

I was in the wheelhouse of the vessel with my partner and the skipper. I informed the skipper that due to the multiple infractions in this case, the entire catch would be seized and charges were forthcoming from this investigation. The skipper turned very red in the face and looked as if he was going to explode. Suddenly, my partners cellular phone started ringing. The cell tone was set to play the tune of the "Lone Ranger Theme song". When this occurred, my partner immediately left the wheelhouse to answer his cell, leaving me with this extremely large and agitated fisherman which exhibited signs of being pushed over the edge of emotion. You had to be there to see the look on this skipper's face when he heard the cell phone tone go off!.

» »   Shot Gun incident   » »

My field trainer told me about this incident to remind me never to get into too many arguments with a member, especially if he constantly disagrees with you. He related that in the early 1990's, at one of the detachments, he had observed two members on a quiet evening arguing over something or other. Apparently this was normal as they never saw eye to eye on anything. Everyone knew they had a healthy, ongoing working rivalry between them. One of the members had enough of the arguments and left the office area only to return a short time later with a 12 gauge shotgun.

He quickly racked a round into the chamber and fired, point blank at his co-worker, yelling something about having had enough of the guy's attitude. Several other members were looking on in horror and paying rigid attention with the sound of shouting and gunfire in the office. The guy without the gun was left still standing in shock. Apparently the first officer had carved the pellets out of the shotgun shell leaving only the cotton wad which hit the second guy in the chest.

» »   Torque Wrench Test   » »

Before the breathalyser instrument was introduced as an investigative tool members would use innovative tools to convince impaired drivers they were being tested. There was word out in the public that the police were about to introduce this new device to combat impaired driving offences. One subject was picked up and in his drunken stupor was given a torque wrench to blow into. The end of the torque wrench had a red light on it so the wrench was set to its lowest setting for torque. The suspect was told to blow into the end unit handle at which time the member just twisted the other end of the wrench and the light came on. The next day when the suspect was brought before the Justice to enter a plea on his charge, the suspect replied "I guess the machine last night said I was drunk." The Justice did not pursue this further but I am sure he knew the investigator had used some sort of trick to convince the suspect he was drunk.

» » You know you're a Cop If... » »

I had a retired member send this list of quotes which made him reflect back on his career and comment that for a good portion of quotes, there were times the member actually felt some of them were exactly the way things were when he was on the road. Some of them a hundred times.

You know you're a cop if...

1) You have the bladder capacity of five people.
2) You have ever restrained someone and it was not a sexual experience.
3) You believe that 50% of people are a waste of good air.
4) Your idea of a good time is a 'man with a gun' call.
5) You conduct a criminal record check on anyone who seems friendly towards you.
6) You believe in the aerial spraying of Prozac and birth control pills.
7) You disbelieve 90% of what you hear and 75% of what you see.
8) You have your weekends off planned for a year.
9) You believe the government should require a permit to reproduce.
10) You refer to your favorite restaurant by the intersection at which it's located.
11) You've had thoughts of wanting to hold a seminar entitled: 'Suicide-Getting it right the first time.'
12) You ever had to put the phone on hold before you begin laughing uncontrollably.
13) You think caffeine should be available in IV form.
14) You believe anyone who says, 'I only had two beers' is going to blow more than a .15 reading.
15) You find out a lot about paranoia just by following people around.

16) Anyone has ever said to you, 'There are people killing other people out there and you are here messing with me.'

17) People flag you down on the street and ask you directions to strange places... and you know where it's located.

18) You can discuss where you are going to eat with your partner while standing over a dead body.

19) You are the only person introduced at social gatherings by profession. (ISN'T THIS THE TRUTH)

20) You walk into places and people think it's high comedy to grab their buddy and shout, 'They've come to get you, Bill.'

21) You do not see daylight from November until May.

22) People shout, 'I didn't do it!' when you walk into a room and think they're being hugely funny and original.

23) A week's worth of laundry consists of 5 T-shirts, 5 pairs of socks, and 5 pairs of underwear.

24) You've ever referred to Tuesday as 'my weekend', or 'this is my Friday'.

25) You've ever written off guns and ammunition as a business deduction.

26) You believe that unspeakable evils will befall you if anyone says, 'Boy it sure is quiet tonight.'

27) Discussing dismemberment over a meal seems perfectly normal to you.

28) You find humor in other people's stupidity.

29) You have left more meals on the restaurant table than you've eaten.

30) You feel good when you hear 'these handcuffs are too tight'.

» » Why I left the Police Service » »

This person was open enough to share her thoughts and now is enjoying her work as a Telecom Operator. Her explanation for leaving the Police Service went as follows:

"I loved being a police officer. My decision to quit the job I was loving and succeeding at was a very difficult one. It all changed when one day I got that knock on the door that no one wants. The police officer, my co-worker – telling me that there had been a death in my family. I was numb. I thought there must be a mistake, but it wasn't. My 17 year old nephew, 8 days from his 18th birthday had been murdered. – A Homicide -, something I had dealt with frequently. The house party gone wrong; The uninvited guests showing up; The party turning violent; - But this time my nephew died. – A good kid. The peacemaker in his group. The one who couldn't get away.

I sought counselling and continued policing for a while. I faked being alright at first. Eventually I was okay with going to the same types of incidents – there was enough of them., But it was always difficult dealing with the victim's family. One day, I attempted a death notification, luckily my co-worker spoke. I could not deliver the news. Watching the reaction of that women when the news was given to her, broke me. I pictured my sister on that day she got the same type of call. That was the day I knew I didn't want to do the job anymore. "Too Close to Home!"

» » Toe Truck requested » »

At an interior BC Detachment, members were dispatched to a call where a guy tried to commit suicide. Upon police arrival, they found the guy missed and shot his toe off. I guess he was checking to see that his rifle was loaded etc. when the incident happened. Asked by dispatch if the members needed and ambulance, the member on scene replied "No, but we could use a "Toe Truck!".

» »   **Act surprised & show concern**   » »

Over the years many members have had discussions about other members getting themselves into trouble which would cause an internal investigation to be conducted. Some would argue that integrity and honesty were always the best thing to fall back on even if it meant accepting responsibility for their actions. Members would state that if you got into shit over something, do the following - "Act surprised, show concern, and deny, deny, deny." This phrase was quite popular amongst members just after the famous murder trial of Saskatchewan's Collin Thatcher who made this statement when accused for being part of a conspiracy to murder his wife. Another version of this was "Claim Ignorance, show remorse and promise it will never happen again."

»» "The morning person" »»

I'm living in the unofficial single men's quarters in a busy northern Alberta town. My roommate, another member, had worked nightshift the day before. Our house was in a rural area and we had been having problems with ground hogs around the house. This particular morning it was quite evident the ground hogs were yelping high pitched sounds at each other, so typical for the prairies. I was upstairs watching TV when I heard my roommate coming upstairs from the basement where the bedrooms were. I looked over and there was my roommate in his underwear with his handgun. He didn't say anything but walked out on the deck and started shooting at the ground hogs. A few seconds later he came back into the house, looked at me, said "Those fricken ground hogs", and went back to bed.

»» "That was a .38!" »»

While stationed in Courtney Detachment we had a call of a man who was reported to be depressed and had gone into a wooded area to do himself in. The NCO I/C of the Detachment quickly arranged search groups to look for the depressed man in the woods. The NCO had all the search groups equipped with portable radios. The NCO was a very nervous type. The Detachment Guard was a seasoned veteran with years of experience around RCMP members, and he had quite a sharp whit.

Over the radio a loud BANG was heard. The NCO immediately got on the air and stated "That sounded like a .38, I'm sure that was a .38. I know a .38 when I hear it!"

There was a pause and a member replied on the radio "No, it was a car backfiring beside me." There was a short pause again but this time the old Guard came on the radio and asked "Could you clarify something, Was that a '38 Ford or a '38 Chev?" There were no further transmissions for a few minutes.

»» "The Shit Theory" »»

A member tries to explain to his new recruit that in their department shit travels down hill. To illustrate this he draws the word in a downward fashion with the letters only.

S

H

I

T …. and makes his point that if you get into shit in this organization, you can pretty well expect more shit to come from the top of the organizations bosses. He then re-enforces the need for making sure one does not get into situations that would get him into "shit".

»» GIS call out »»

A telecom Operator explains how she had to deal with a GIS (General Investigation Section) member when she decided to call him in the middle of the night. This might explain why sometimes a member doesn't respond to a call as quickly as we'd like them to:

I called out "Pat", our "on call" GIS member, for an armed robbery that had just taken place at a local cold beer and wine store. We're a small detachment so our GIS doesn't work 24 hrs. Pat answers the phone and I give him the details of the call and he says "yeah, I'll be right there!" So about ½ hour goes by and he hasn't shown up. I call him on the radio and finally get a response "I'll be right in there to see you." Seems Pat had a little trouble "coming around" out of his sleep. He explained that he got out of bed and went right for his closet. He's standing inside his closet so his wife, who was woken up by the phone as well, goes to see what he's doing in there. She caught him just before he pee'd all over their clothes so she directs him into the bathroom where he starts to wake up. His adrenaline starts going and he's off to the races and flies out of the house like a mad man. He jumps in his truck, in the garage, hits reverse and runs over their dog, who was sleeping in the garage. The dog was fine, got only his tail. This story cracks me up because I'm sure everyone who has ever been called out of a dead sleep can relate to it.

FINAL THOUGHTS

I hope you have enjoyed this book as much as I have enjoyed putting it together. There are hundreds of stories that have not been told and may only be shared by those who meet as colleagues to reminisce once more in their coffee klatches.

My neighbour recently presented me with a small plaque he purchased at a garage sale for twenty five cents. The inscription is my parting thought for those who enjoyed this book.

R.J. (Bob) Rogalski
E-Mail: rogy1@shaw.ca

old
policemen
never die —
they just
get a charge
out of things!

"WHAT COPS TALK ABOUT OVER COFFEE!"

We know you have thoroughly enjoyed reading "What Cops Talk About Over Coffee!" and that you will want to order copies for your friends and family. This book will make a wonderful

Christmas Gift

Birthday Gift

Father's Day Gift

Mother's Day Gift

Police Academy Graduation Gift

Any Occasion Gift

Also available in e-book form

Volume II of What Cops Talk About Over Coffee contains a further collection of memories from the 1950's to 2012.

www.ingramcontent.com/pod-product-compliance
Lightning Source LLC
LaVergne TN
LVHW021658060526
838200LV00050B/2404